Adventures in
Leninland

An Intrepid Journalist's Quest to Understand a Place Once Called The Soviet Union

Adventures in Leninland

An Intrepid Journalist's Quest to Understand a Place Once Called The Soviet Union

J. Ajlouny

Fresh Ink Group
Guntersville

ADVENTURES IN LENINLAND
An Intrepid Journalist's Quest
To Understand a Place
Once Called the Soviet Union

Copyright © 2018, 1999, 1989
by J. Ajlouny
All rights reserved

Fresh Ink Group
An Imprint of:
The Fresh Ink Group, LLC
Box 931
Guntersville, AL 35976
Email: info@FreshInkGroup.com
FreshInkGroup.com

Edition 1.0   1989
Edition 2.0   1999
Edition 3.0   2018

3.0 book design by Thelma Khan

Except as permitted under the U.S. Copyright Act of 1976, no part of this publication may be reproduced, distributed, or transmitted in any form or by any means, or stored in a database or retrieval system, without prior written permission of the Fresh Ink Group, LLC.

BISAC Subject Headings:
TRV023000 **TRAVEL** / Russia
HIS032000 **HISTORY** / Russia & the Former Soviet Union
BIO023000 **BIOGRAPHY & AUTOBIOGRAPHY** / Adventurers & Explorers

Library of Congress Control Number: 2018901426

ISBN-13: 978-1-936442-99-7 Papercover
ISBN-13: 978-1-936442-98-0 Hardcover
ISBN-13: 978-1-936442-97-3 Ebooks

To all those communists who were swallowed
by the system they helped, in good faith, create

and

To all the innocent victims who,
through no fault of their own,
were swallowed by it.

Contents

PART I

IDEAS

The Lenin Mausoleum 11

The Times Are A Changin' 13

You've Come A Long Way Babushka. 17

Stalin On Trial? 21

Disclosing The Names, Counting The Numbers 25

Even The Names Are Changing 29

Socialism Today 33

Socialism Tomorrow 39

History As Lies 43

PART II

PEOPLE

Gorby, We Hardly Know Ya' 53

The Mystic of Moscow 59

Where Were You When Stalin Died? 65

Molotov: The Last of The Lambs 73

Boris The Bold 79

Requiem for A Lightweight 85

PART III

PLACES

Arbat: The Soviet Soho 93

The Art of Smuggling 97

Moldavia Daze 101
Honor Eternal 107
Odessa: The Red Black Seaport 115
They Came to Stay 119

PART IV

POLITICS

The Year 1989 125
The Year 1990. 135
Upwardly Mobile Communists Stand By Their Party 141

PART V

ODDITIES

Death in The U.S.S.R.. 149
Vacation Time Is All Timing. 151
It's a Dog's Life 155
Buying New Car Takes Patience or Luck. 157
Strange Prohibitions And Glasnost Spur New Defiance. 161
Panda-Monium 165
Adventures at the New Age Summit. 169
Tanks A Million. 175

PART VI

The Hunt for Gorbachev's House 179

Preface and Acknowledgements

Though it is not customary to combine these two elements of a book, I chose to do so because so much of what I have to say is one long story. Dividing it into too many parts would only muddy the plot.

These essays and articles were written in a period of four years 1988-1991, during which I visited the Soviet Union three times. Many of them were published in newspapers and magazines around the world after a London-based syndication service agreed to distribute them on its newswires. Others were written for specific publications. Still others never saw the light of day. Those that have been selected for inclusion in this volume touched me most deeply or were the most fun to write and, hopefully, to read.

Many thanks are in order. My parents and my sisters deserve the highest appreciation for supporting and encouraging their idealistic son and brother in these endeavors. Thanks are also owed to my friend Vladimir Zaretsky of the Information Department of the Soviet Embassy in Washington, D.C. His assistance in fulfilling my travel itineraries was nothing short of heroic. Victor Karasin, the managing editor of *Soviet Life* magazine deserves praise for publishing some of these articles and photographs, as well as for granting me the permission to reprint writings and photographs from his fine publication and to the Novosti Press Agency, which granted me a journalism fellowship that enabled me to travel so widely and meet so many Soviet citizens.

Thanks also to Lisa McDonald, my trusted typist and some-time editor; to Thelma Kahn who designed the book; to June Parker for preparing the illustrations; to Berg Djelderian for creating the cover as I envisioned it; and to Dina Dalaly, Renee Cooper, Tempest Moore, Matthew Harb, for inspiration, and for granting me leave to complete it.

Introduction

I compiled the diverse writings in this volume primarily for the benefit of my family and friends. I was continually asked to explain my interest — my fascination — with the Soviet Union. I was also asked to expound upon the many interesting and queer things I found there. Despite their encouragement, I kept putting this task off, declining to yield to the self-flattery it necessarily entailed. They denied this would be so. In fact my father actually offered to pay to have these essays published if I would just re-edit them. In the end, like Shakespeare's portrayal of Julius Caesar I succumbed to the myth that the highest form of flattery is being told you cannot be flattered.

To answer the first question, I can clearly discern the two events which prompted me to commence my admittedly non-academic study of the Union of Soviet Socialist Republics (U.S.S.R.), and Communism generally. A third event caused me to reinforce my belief in these subjects. It was August 1980 and I was in London visiting friends. While enjoying drinks and friendly company at a pub beside the Thames the name Alexander Dubček1 came up in conversation. I had not heard the name before but all those I was with certainly had. I felt embarrassed and ashamed of my ignorance. I knew then and there that I wanted to know all about him. For a person who always prided himself on his general knowledge of world history, it was a momentous awakening.

Shortly thereafter, while in graduate school I had the opportunity to read an account of the Stalin show trials of the mid-1930's. I was completely dumbstruck that tried and true communist revolutionaries could be found guilty of committing the most heinous state crimes based solely upon confession evidence which was absolutely absurd. How could such a thing have happened? How could one man - Stalin - get away with so many lies and so many deaths without incurring the wrath of his colleagues? Only God will ever know the true pain of the lives that were shattered in his effort to expose so-called "enemies of the people." After that I was hooked. I wanted to understand how so much calculated cruelty could befall so many people. Remember, Stalin and the Stalinists of the Soviet Union's Eastern European allies butchered their own people, not others.

Over the following decade, I was a voracious consumer of books and information about the Soviet Union, her people and her Warsaw Pact neighbors. I made several trips there, one of which was an extended tour of more than a hundred cities and towns. I visited the former German Democratic Republic, crossed over and under the Berlin Wall, and arranged excursions to Poland, Hungary and Czechoslovakia. It's a world which has since disappeared... and changed, hopefully for the better.

I became a walking encyclopedia of facts and stories about the 1917 Revolution, the Russian Civil War, the period between the wars, and about the Soviet struggle against Nazi Germany. I attempted to understand Stalin's paranoia, as well as Khrushchev's reaction to it. I closely followed the last years of the Brezhnev regime, and got up early to watch his, Andropov's and Chernenko's funerals on American television. Despite my thoughts in Part II's "Gorby, We Hardly Know Ya'," I quickly saw Gorbachev as a new breed of Communist leader. I had seen him a year before he assumed power during his visit to the city of Windsor in Ontario, Canada, where he toured, among other places, a historic liquor distillery. I was able to shake his hand and I have since obtained his autograph on the cover of the *Time* magazine that named him Man of the Year for 1987. I even founded the short-lived Mikhail Gorbachev Fan Club of North America to "Rally Around Mikhail." I was not particularly fond of him. I simply admired his courage and gave him credit for changing the face of the world. Whatever can be said against him, he deserves at least that consideration. Boris Yeltsin also deserves credit for being more willing than Gorbachev to shake off the shackles of

Communism. I once met him, accidentally and very briefly while on a Moscow subway car. He was Moscow Party Chief then and a candidate member of the Politburo. Gorbachev promoted the man who most acutely engineered his downfall. How ironic.

The third event I mentioned above which confirmed my devotion to "all things Soviet" was the sudden, frenetic manner in which its empire collapsed. Dissent, once a dangerous practice, was proliferated literally overnight throughout the lands behind the fabled Iron Curtain. People who were afraid to speak only weeks before were quickly drowning in each others accusations. Hard-nosed Communists seemingly disappeared for fear of experiencing the peoples' wrath. A world which took 45 years to shape was suddenly transformed in a matter of months. The year 1989 will be as significant in world history as 1215, 1492, 1776, and 1945 are. If asked I would describe it as "the year the world turned right."

The essays I have included herein are the product of my experiences and observations in the Soviet Union. I hope you will read them as they were written: seriously, but with the intention to inform and entertain, and ultimately to satisfy the curiosity and stimulate the minds of those closest to me. I wrote many more but I had difficulty locating them. For those that are re-printed here, I kept them relatively short and to the point.

Most people don't know (or remember) that I once wrote a comic strip called *Party Ranks* that parodied life in the bureaucracy of the Soviet Communist Party. It was a harebrained idea but I figured I might be able to traffic in my knowledge and interest in this subject by injecting a measure of wit and humor into the fray. And for the most part it worked. To amplify the absurdity of my view, I set the strip in the fictional Banners and Slogans Division of the mythical Propaganda Ministry. I wanted *Party Ranks* to do for the U.S.S.R. what *Hogan's Heroes* did to the Nazis.

Set in the mythical Banners & Slogans Department of the fictional Propaganda Ministry, Party Ranks was my attempt to highlight the absurdities of the Cold War. It was syndicated to newspapers serving U.S. military bases around the world by an Edinburgh, Scotland-based features syndicate 1984-86. My inspiration was the ratcheting-up of anti-Soviet sentiment in the West following the downing of Korean Air Lines Flight 007 west of Sakhalin in the Sea of Japan in September 1983. Despite my expectation it would become a worldwide sensation, the strip sputtered out of existence following the reform policies of Mikhail Gorbachev.

With Reagan-era ratcheting up of dormant Cold War tensions, I had big hopes of success. I predicted every newspaper daily in the USA would run my strip and I would certainly be invited to all the late-night talk shows and be interviewed on NPR programs. I figured a TV series was within the realm of possibilities and I fantasized about sunning myself on a *Party Ranks* beach towel while sipping tea from a *Party Ranks* coffee mug. All I needed was a big features syndicate to share my vision. Instead I got a dinky syndicate from Edinburgh, Scotland to distribute *Party Ranks* to newspapers in Europe, South Korea, The Philippines and other places that served USA military bases. I begrudgingly acknowledged an international promotional tour was not in the picture.

Like the CIA itself, I didn't fathom Gorbachev's reforms would send the Soviet empire into ruin. So my dream of becoming another Charles Schultz was dashed by the time 1991 ended and the U.S.S.R. ceased to exist. It's just as well. I always felt a little guilty about poking fun at a system that ostensibly promised an end to war, injustice, exploitation and discrimination; a system that has at its core the Christian values of sharing and equality. If only it worked out that way.

[1.] Dubček was the First Secretary of the Czechoslovak Communist Party who ushered in the first real reforms to Stalinist-style rule there in 1968, a period which has been labeled the Prague Spring. He was quickly deposed following an invasion by Czechoslovakia's "allies" in the Warsaw Pact. He lived the next two decades in virtual obscurity, but in 1989 went public again to support his countrymen's demands for a "Velvet Revolution." He was appointed Chairman of the Federal Assembly of Czechoslovakia in 1989. That's what communists call "rehabilitation."

Part I

IDEAS

The Lenin Mausoleum at the Kremlin Wall in Moscow's historic Red Square. This photograph was taken on March 10, 1953 during Josef Stalin's funeral procession. Pictured on the platform are members of the Politburo of the Soviet Communist Party Central Committee. The Mausoleum was erected in 1927, three years after his death. Stalin's name and groomed corpse were removed in 1957, following his denunciation by Nikita Khrushchev in his so-called "Secret Speech" to a gathering of the Communist Party elite. A year later, his remains were buried in a grave beneath the Kremlin wall, next to the remains of other revolutionary leaders. It was a demotion that remains controversial even today.

THE LENIN MAUSOLEUM

Will It Survive? Does it deserve to?

Mikhail Gorbachev's reforms were supposed to unfold in a controlled manner. Glasnost would slowly pave the way to democracy; Perestroika would eventually produce a market economy. Stalin, Brezhnev and Chernenko were discredited. Khrushchev and Andropov were acclaimed. Vladimir Lenin, the Washington, Jefferson and Lincoln of the U.S.S.R., would remain untouched, and therefore unjudged by revisionist (truthful!) historians. That was the plan anyway. Events in the Soviet Union and Eastern Europe have unraveled so rapidly and haphazardly that even Lenin's generation is not expected to survive. To many this consequence would be welcome, but others would bitterly contest any such suggestion. Lenin, as the founder of the Soviet state, was an honest revolutionary whose only aim was to liberate workers and peasants from exploitation. But can his excesses be forgiven?

This argument is unpersuasive to millions of former Communist subjects across Eastern Europe. Publicly displayed statues, busts and murals of Lenin are disappearing faster than they were erected. And that's pretty fast! Lenin's voluminous writings are being systematically attacked by those who literally yesterday extolled their virtues. Street names, central squares and parks named in his honor have been discreetly renamed. As a result, it is safe to conclude that Lenin, beyond the borders of the U.S.S.R., is history.

But what about within the Soviet Union itself? Can Lenin survive? Will thousands still stand in line for hours across Red Square to visit his ostentatious tomb? Even more seriously: Should the tomb be closed and his body finally interred in the hallowed Russian soil? These are questions I asked on a sunny afternoon in Red Square while waiting my turn to pass before the glass-encased Communist. The line was so incredibly long that I had plenty of time to conduct my little poll.

Most people said Lenin was still the architect of the nation and should be respected as such. "He was our liberator, our leader," one man said. "He died too early," said another. "There is no telling where he could have led us." Stalin, not Lenin, was widely believed to be responsible for their country's plight. Yet surprisingly, a simple majority claimed to have no objection to closing his mausoleum. A woman said they ought to burn the body first. She, like an increasing number of others, sees Lenin as the symbol of the Communist system everyone is determined to abolish. Yet the line of people waiting to visit his glass-encased corpse never ceases to be anything other than very, very long; a pilgrimage to an idea, perhaps, more than a man.

A young lady from Minsk then said, "I don't care if they move him or keep in there, just don't wake him up!"

THE TIMES ARE A CHANGIN'

Yesterday's Dreams (and Nightmares) Are Today's Realities?

The Iron Curtain is now irretrievably drawn. The Warsaw Pact, that once feared amalgamation of men, missiles and tanks, is in disarray and will not likely survive an integrated Europe. Democratically elected governments have replaced the totalitarian regimes of the Soviet Union and its fraternal Socialist allies. The Berlin Wall is largely rubble, the stuff of speculators and museum curators. In short, the Cold War, the ideological rivalry between the forces of Capitalism represented by the U.S. and those of Communism as represented by the U.S.S.R., is over. Good riddance is the universal refrain.

In the wake of the startling developments across Eastern Europe, many have begun to wonder whether the world is a safer or more dangerous place. That World War II has finally come to an end appears to be clear beyond doubt. The reunification of Germany in October, 1990 and the signing of the Paris Charter of the Conference for Security and Cooperation in Europe (CSCE) in the Spring of 1991 saw to this. The Cold War was the last (and longest) battle of that horrendous conflagration. But where will it lead us? Is the promise of the 21st century in sight or are we deluding ourselves in hoping so? These are questions that command lengthy deliberation.

Philosophy aside, a glance across the spectrum of the once divided continent leads one to believe President George Bush's fabled New World Order might yield a New World Disorder instead. Like the storm-tossed summit of Malta in December 1989, the outlook is both hopeful and foreboding. Mikhail Gorbachev must have been more than a little seasick.

Like the Berlin Wall before it, the Soviet Union is crumbling before our very eyes. Like all the new democracies of Europe it is an economic basket-case and a cauldron of long suppressed ethnic and territorial antagonisms. The dream of political freedom and human rights has been burst by a laundry list of problems: Bankruptcy, corruption, pollution, unemployment, crime, rebellion and nationalistic fervor. Gorbachev's reforms have done more short-term harm than good. The result is a drama not even Tolstoy could have penned.

An inventory of their problems, however, shouldn't have obscured the significant changes that have taken place since Communism collapsed so swiftly, so soundly. Apart from holding nominally democratic elections, the parliaments of these nations have passed sweeping reform laws granting, among other things, freedom of expression, freedom to worship, to travel, to vote and freedom to own private property. Censorship of the press and in the arts has all but ended. Artists and writers are now free to follow their inspirations. Rock music and adult magazines are now available for enjoyment from formally East Berlin to Vladivostok. A free economy based upon the profit motive has begun to take shape. Initiative in personal and public affairs is being encouraged, and sometimes rewarded. Various groups are organizing, there are now dozens of political parties where there was only one last year. All in all, it's a remarkable list of achievements, at least as formidable as their list of problems.

One Polish reformer summed it up best when he said, "First you get the freedom, then you get the headaches."

GDR Girl

Upon the cobbled streets of
    Leipzig, old Leipzig
Puffing heavy in a soft coal
    dark hard dialectic smoke
Past windows peeking dim from
    flat and tower
Where constellations blink in
    the fogs of national power
State secrets, in official cloak,
    dress strategically pink:
The girls of the GDR
    a special Saxon breed
Democratically romantic
Lustily pedantic
Fervent, warm, and frantic
With heat and hold and creed
Schooled to mend a cog, to fix
    a sprocket
To sail a boat, to load and
    dock it
Arrayed on assembly lines,
    each is eminently quick
And the hair, extraordinarily thick
Conserved in a bun flows down
    when the quota is met
Come home GDR girl, with
    graphs of strong production
And the smile no government
    could genetically set
And talk your talk, that red seduction
Until morning when the sky
    is bright with possibility
And field and machines await your touch
The softness, ideology and such
And I am gone across a wall,
    flying like a propaganda dove
Hoping you, exile from freedom
Remember me, exile from love

YOU'VE COME A LONG WAY BABUSHKA

Soviet Feminists Face a Long Road Despite Gains

Orel: Though the stereotypical picture of Soviet women is either a babushka-clad war widow or fat matron standing in a breadline, the first ruminations of a women's rights movement is beginning to be heard. Inspired by Glasnost and fueled by Perestroika, women all over the U.S.S.R. are beginning to organize under the banner of better working conditions, more food and consumer goods in stores and perhaps most importantly, for greater respect for machismo Soviet maledom.

Valerina Basharina, deputy editor in chief of *Rabottnitsa* (Working Woman) magazine, the Soviet Union's largest circulation women's weekly, addressed these and other issues facing her countrywomen at a recent university seminar in Detroit, Michigan. "While women face many problems peculiar to their gender," she said, "the majority of what ails them ails everybody in Soviet society."

"There is an ill economy and a lack of respect for individual rights which leads to great difficulties for the entire people," she told those gathered to hear her address. "The most important thing is to provide both men and women with equal rights under the law, and to have that law enforced."

An American author who also spoke to the conference, which was entitled: *Women's Rights and Gorbachev's Reforms*, reported that Soviet women have had to begin their struggle for rights without information or books of similar movements in the West. Francine du Plessix Gray, author of the new book *Soviet Women: Walking the Tightrope*, said an old-fashioned form of male-created Puritanism, adopted and reinforced by Communism, is the largest obstacle to women's rights. She reported: "The government has never sanctioned an analysis of gender roles in the U.S.S.R. for fear of upsetting its Marxist class ideology."

- Among the most pressing problems facing Soviet women today include:
- A dysfunctional healthcare system that suffers from shortages of hospital beds and medicines.
- Scarcity of contraceptive devices, which has led to the highest reported abortion rate of any country. The average Soviet woman will have seven abortions in her lifetime.
- An outdated economy which requires most women to work outside the house (92 percent) many whom are employed in what is customarily defined as "man's labor," such as mining, factory work and farming.
- A culture where men refuse to help around the house or in raising their own children.
- Waiting in long lines to shop for everything from eggs to soap, a process which eats up almost four hours of every woman's day.

"The economic situation is such that it eats up women's time and energy," said Basharina. "It is bad for families, bad for society. The woman has no right to choose what she wants. She's forced to live a double-role of working and running a household. In a recent poll in our magazine (circulation 25 million) we found that 20 percent of our readers would prefer to just be homemakers, and 20 percent wish they could have their careers. The rest would combine both family and career but confessed to be unable to adequately do either."

"It's one of our most important priorities," added Basharina, "because Gorbachev has said that the way for women must be opened from top to bottom. The cultural level of society is related to the cultural level of its women. We wish more of our men were like Gorbachev!"

Though the Soviet Union was the first government to grant female emancipation into its constitution, attempts to implement that policy were largely failures. Stalin's reactionary policies and the teaming Soviet bureaucracy are the chief culprits. The promise of free healthcare, childcare facilities and government provided sanatoriums has apparently not yielded the expected benefits.

Basharina noted that the new Soviet parliament has introduced several new laws aimed at curing many of women's concerns. Greater job-protection, maternity leave and tougher child-support enforcement are just a few of the measures currently being debated. "And for the first-time issues like domestic violence and birth-control are being freely discussed. We're thankful we can at least start to talk about these things," she said.

Valerina Basharina flanked by two colleagues. "Women's concerns are national conerns," she insists.
Photo by author

Hour Glass by Pyotr Belov, 1987. This is one of a dozen posters commissioned by Memorial for the opening of the exhibition organized to commemorate the victims of Stalin's repression. Even today, a vocal minority does its best to preserve the memory of Josef Stalin and hold an annual birthday celebration in his honor in his birthplace Gori, Georgia, where a museum to his life remains a popular tourist attraction.

STALIN ON TRIAL?

Memorial Organization Will Try to Do That and More

Smolensk: A sure sign that the Soviet Union is on its way to renewal can be found in the newly formed organization Memorial, described as a historical and educational society formed to expose the crimes of Stalinism. In pre-Glasnost times, such a group would be unthinkable. Its meetings would be sacked and its members charged with crimes like Anti-State Activities and Anti-Soviet Slander, and the like. Dangerous ideas, such as the truth, could not be tolerated in a totalitarian society.

That Stalin and his henchmen were a lawless gang was officially admitted in 1956 during Khrushchev's famous secret speech before the 20th Party Congress. Yet the extent and cost of the repression remained a taboo subject. Though it was known many innocent people were condemned to death, it was not known whom, nor how many met this fate. Even Khrushchev's six-hour speech that night failed to mention Stalin's war against the people. His condemnations were directed primarily against Stalin's crimes against the Communist Party, violations of socialist legality and his incompetent handling of the Great Patriotic War which caused the Soviet Union's horrific losses.

Today Memorial seeks to fill that void. It recently sponsored Memory Week (March 1989) in honor of all the victims of the "Cult of Personality," the common term used to describe the era of the dictatorship of Josef Stalin (1924-1953). In April it held its first public exhibition of a Mourning Wall, a large room with its walls covered with the photographs, reportorial accounts, death certificates and rehabilitation decrees from the Military Collegium of the Supreme Court of the U.S.S.R. exonerating the victims of Stalin's mass terror. It was by all accounts a silent and gut-wrenching experience.

For the first time ever, reliable statistics are being accumulated from hundreds of long-closed government archives. Numbers which started in the thousands have grown to millions. Beginning in 1927, with the forced collectivization of Soviet agriculture, Stalin and the NKVD (the pre-1946 acronym for the Peoples' Commissariat for Internal Affairs, today the MVD Ministry of Internal Affairs), systematically "liquidated" several million private farming families. Their tactics were sickeningly simple: Outright murder, enforced starvation or mass deportation to labor camps. Then in the mid-1930's Stalin swung his axe over the Communist Party itself. Between 1935 and 1939 he had thousands of high and low Party officials executed on trumped up charges of disloyalty. Respected Communists, many who personally played significant roles in the 1917 Revolution, were humiliated in public show trials and hung or shot depending on their ranks. Stalin also gutted the Soviet military of more than half of its officer-class between 1937 and 1939. Not only was it a cruel and immoral act, it also cost the Soviet Union dearly when Nazi Germany was invaded in June 1941.

But peasants, government, Party and military officials were not the least of Stalin's victims. Hundreds of thousands of ordinary citizens were erroneously labeled "Enemies of the People" and condemned to death or long sentences in the Gulags of Siberia. Uncounted thousands of writers, composers, filmmakers, artists, historians, professors, trade unionists, and untold others shared a similar fate. It was a time accurately defined as "The Rule of the Meat Grinder." How one man could command so much violence is unclear. The fact is he succeeded. Memorial was established to make sure such a time never happens again.

Victoria Chalikova is a writer, member of Memorial and passionate speaker on the subject of uncovering Stalin's crimes. She explained the enormous popularity of Memorial's agenda as the peoples' yearning for justice. "Though the victims and their executioners are long gone, we cannot accept what was done in the name of Socialism because we know it was false. We have a burning desire to hear the whole horrible truth," she said. A man with a placard around his neck passed Chalikova. The placard contains the names and photos of his parents, one of a million couples that disappeared a generation ago. He is searching for any clues about their eventual fate. Chalikova continued: "A person's life is not complete unless he learns what happened to his family. The void into which so many of our people were born is dark and foreboding. Those who visit the Wall cannot leave without being changed forever."

Exposing Stalin's crimes is not Memorial's only goal. It is demanding his body be removed from the Kremlin Wall. Posthumous expulsion from the Party followed by an indictment and trial are also demanded. It also wants the state's role in the mass repression fully disclosed. All victims are to be rehabilitated and their survivors compensated. All accomplices are to be condemned and reviled. The group is organizing a fund drive to establish a memorial complex to the victims of Stalinism too. Chalikova predicts Memorial will accomplish each of these goals, but it will take along time she said.

Journalist Olga Nemirovskaya recently wrote that Memory Week, "resounded nationwide to signal the reappraisal of Stalinism. We have enough evidence on which to base our verdict. We are all the victims of Stalinism, both former prisoners and those who were never arrested. We will be unable to change Soviet ethics and revive our state until we get Stalinism out of our system."

Memorial's co-chair is Yuri Afanasyev, a noted historian and adviser to President Gorbachev. He told *Soviet Life* Magazine that the denunciation of Stalin was a reaction to the peoples' fear of terror and arbitrary rule. "Memorial is a historical, political cultural and juridical movement. Our main task is to revive the social consciousness of the community in order to cast off the evil spell of Stalinism," he said. "But a socially active will never emerge unless cooperation among people with different views replaces the make-believe unity we used to boast about."

The great Russian linguist Averintsev likened the act of commemoration as a symbolic gesture of our faith in the mystical unity of generations. That's the way everything in nature is planned: The roots are in the ground, the leaves are in the sun. That's a thought one cannot easily forget while gazing at the many faces upon the Mourning Wall.

DISCLOSING THE NAMES, COUNTING THE NUMBERS

Young Archivist's Obsession with the Condemned Gets Criticism and Acclaim

Leningrad: Dimitri Yurasov is not unlike any 28 year-old Soviet man. He has an incomplete education, a low-paying job and he knows when to keep his mouth closed. But Yurasov has an unusual hobby. Since the age of 15 he has devoted himself entirely to compiling an index of the innocent victims of Stalin's repression. He has more than 20,000 names (and their stories) in his collection, and it continues to grow. He tends to be a little more serious than most people his generation.

Yurasov's fascination with Stalin's victims began when he encountered the relatively common phrase "unlawfully convicted and posthumously rehabilitated" in Soviet history books following people's names. Who were these people? How and why were they condemned? These are

Since the advent of Glasnost, historians and researchers such as Dimitri Yurasov have devoted themselves to uncovering long held secrets in old secret Soviet archives.

questions he's asked himself ever since. Short stints at several different government archives only strengthened his determination. His hobby resulted in his firing for each such position. His passion for identifying and documenting names caused him to neglect his studies and he was expelled from the university.

It was at a conference of Moscow's Writers Union that young Yurasov decided to divulge his conclusions. The evening was devoted to an examination of life in the 1930's. Stalin's crimes were the main focus. When the speaker declined to quantify the extent of the terror, Yurasov jumped up and cried, "I have statistics!" It was a declaration which changed his life.

The tall and surly archivist has since traveled around the country giving speeches in which he reveals the highest file number he saw was number 16,000,000. His own catalog of names numbers 125,000. He has found a new job and has re-enrolled in school. His courageous exploits were recently the subject of a television documentary. He is a hero to millions of his countrymen. Thousands seek him out to inquire whether his index contains information about their long lost loved ones.

Each story is a dramatic episode. Writer Victoria Chalikova related one told to Yurasov that is particularly poignant:

> *"Dimitri found my father in his catalog, named the camp he had been sent to and where he probably died. But that's not all. Dimitri copied a summary of eyewitness accounts from the rehabilitation file. From one of them I learned that my father had been referred to as "The Librarian." Whether that was a camp nickname or his vocation I don't know. But when he said it, my heart missed a beat. For me he suddenly became real. From the anonymous gray mass of prisoners he stood out in sharp profile—my father was a librarian. It was really something.*

Once Yurasov completes his research on the bloody 1930's he promised to tackle the even bloodier 1940's. Don't expect him to finish anytime soon.

EVEN THE NAMES ARE CHANGING

Towns, Factories and Street Names Follow Communism's Downfall

Moscow: One of the more interesting by-products of Mikhail Gorbachev's reforms is a new penchant to restore the pre-revolutionary names of hundreds of cities and towns. In a country like the Soviet Union, where almost every street, building, school, theater, station and factory is named in honor of one hero or another, this is proving to be quite an undertaking.

Seen by many as a facet of Perestroika, a national conference was recently held in Moscow to discuss this very topic. By all accounts, it was a stormy gathering.

Backed by a vocal group of historians, geographers, linguists and urban planners, a proposal to rename about 20 large cities was taken up by the attendees at the 1st All-Union Conference on Toponymy, which met in Moscow this past April (sic. 1989). The renaming furor was buoyed by the results of an opinion poll in the Russian city of Gorky which showed 90 percent of its residents wanted the historical name - Nizhny Novgorod- restored. But Gorky officials balked at the move in the face of prepared estimates which pegged the cost at between 50 and 60 million roubles. At a meeting of the City Soviet (Soviet means "Workers' Council"), the question was put to the deputies between the renaming of the city or the construction of a new housing project. They chose the housing project.

Critics of the Gorky decision say the estimates were ridiculously overstated. Many see the resistance not as a matter of money, but as a combination of personal and political fear of initiative which runs contrary to Gorbachev's spirit of reform. Similar accusations have been tossed back and forth in cities, towns and villages all around the country. In essence, it is a question like so many others which have arisen under Gorbachev: The old against the new; the Party against the reformers; Brezhnevism versus Gorby-mania. It's not hard to guess who will win.

The Soviet Cultural Foundation, a bastion of Glasnost inspired intellectuals, estimates that more than one hundred localities have already restored their old names. These are mostly small towns and rural collective farms and so cost was not a major inhibition. Thus, Gheorghiu-Dezh in Khazakistan will become Liski again. Kirovobad in Uzbekistan is now restored to Gzhatsk. Soon the rebuilt Leninabad in Armenia, the epicenter of December 1988's earthquake, will once again become Khodzhen, a name which local historians claim is more than 2,500 years old.

In 1986, a decree of the Supreme Soviet, the country's highest governmental authority, automatically restored the old names to all towns, farms, streets and squares named after Leonid Brezhnev and Konstantin Chernenko. These two former Party leaders are now officially in disgrace and have therefore forfeited their rights to be publicly honored. So says the government. Perhaps the most famous city renaming took place in 1961, when the city of Stalingrad became Volgograd. This was a decision taken in the old way; it was adopted in secret by the Politburo without any forewarning. The decision was implemented overnight!

But like all the changes happening in the Soviet Union today, caution is the key word. Cartographers claim their work would be thrown into a tizzy if hundreds of towns, roads and stations are renamed to settle political scores. They know that the potential number of changes could raise to several thousand. Russian nationalists, on the other hand, see the movement as an attack on their very honor. To them, the entire Gorbachev era has been a tremendous disappointment, even a threat. They suggest that the dropping of revolutionary names and titles is an admission of failure. This is a prospect which many are unwilling to countenance.

Their critics are quick to label them as reactionaries and Stalinists. They wonder how many Kirovs, Octoberists, Sovietsks and Krasnaya (red) this and thats can be tolerated? It's bad enough having streets named things like, The Avenue of Metallurgical Engineers and Young Pioneer Parkway, without having factories named, for example, The Rosa Luxembourg

Contraceptives Cooperative and the January Uprising Plant.

The renaming controversy is bound to continue. It is but another symptom of the overwhelming dissatisfaction the people have of their government and economic conditions. On its surface it is not as vital an issue as, for instance, the nationalities question on food shortages, or the adoption of native languages and flags, but it will be a festering subject of debate for a long time to come.

Only when Leningrad is restored to Petrograd or St. Petersburg will the process ever be complete.

SOCIALISM TODAY

Does it Have a Future?

Nikolai Shishlin

There's one thing you can say for Fidel Castro. He's got guts! The embattled Cuban dictator has vowed to stay the course of Marxist orthodoxy in spite of all the evidence which proves its failure. The Cuban economy is all the evidence he could need.

It can't be easy for a generation of battle-hardened ideologues to give up their dreams of a Communist Utopia. Castro is not alone in clinging to the old system. Ardent Communists sit in the legislatures of all the newly liberated states of Eastern Europe, though none call themselves Communists anymore. Gorbachev remains the General Secretary of the Communist Party of the Soviet Union. China seems determined to maintain its Marxist-Maoist line.

But even so, Communism as we've known is, it as President Reagan prophesized, "destined for the ash heap of history." The Marxist-

Leninist model as shaped by Stalin is no more. Notwithstanding their protestations, both Cuba and China have already instituted economic changes to conform to the new world reality. North Korea not so much. The question arises: Does the collapse of Communism signal the failure of Socialism too?

Who better to address this issue than Nikolai Shishlin, a Soviet Central Committee member and director of its International Economic Relations subcommittee. His views on the outlook for international Socialism were first carried by the government newspaper *Izvestia*, and subsequently reprinted in *Soviet Life* Magazine (March 1990), which kindly granted its permission to reproduce it here. (Shishlin has been a regular talking head on ABC's Nightline and PBS's the MacNeil-Lerher Report and other Western media outlets.)

What are the recent political developments in Eastern Europe among the Soviet Union's Warsaw Pact allies?

Poland, Hungary, the German Democratic Republic, Bulgaria, Czechoslovakia, and Romania have entered into a period of radical reforms. It is noted everywhere that the Soviet Union not only hailed and supported the revolutionary changes happening in the Warsaw Treaty countries, but also encouraged them by its policy of Perestroika and its unconditional denunciation of the Stalinist model of Socialism.

It is more or less clear what the Eastern European countries want to break with. They have said No to the administrative-command system and the one-party monopoly on power. They have said No to ideological dogmatism and the system of power that ignore the fundamental laws of economic and political development. They have said No to dishonest, corrupt, and immoral leaders who usurped the right to declare what was right and what was wrong on behalf of the party and the people. They have said "No" to many things, so I repeat, this is more or less clear.

Where do you believe these changes will lead them?

Other questions are far more difficult to answer: Where are the Eastern European countries heading? How will their social systems develop? What factors will dominate the development of what has recently been referred to as the "socialist community" and the "nucleus of the world socialist system"?

Answers to these questions are coming both from people who are directly involved in the stormy process of renewal and from sideline spectators who are watching the swift change of characters and events.

In a nutshell, the points of view fall into several categories: First, Socialism has suffered a defeat. Communist ideology is dead. The only possible future is a return to the bourgeois-democratic system. In other words, onward to the past.

Second, permit me to express a less categorical opinion. In the international dispute between the Communists and the Social-Democrats, who were so zealously and ardently condemned and discredited during Stalin's time and later, the Social-Democrats have ultimately won. That is why, they say, social-democratic methods should be used to cure the ills of the Eastern European countries.

Third, the revolutionary changes in Eastern Europe will cleanse the socialist ideal and rid it of the tragic follies of kleptocratic Socialism. Newly found freedom will enable Eastern Europeans to make a quick recovery, to discard false values, and to embrace the true values of Socialism.

Is there a sense of frustration among your colleagues about the failures your economies have experienced?

All these points of view have a right to exist, but I don't think it's correct to attempt to map out a single course for all of the socialist countries that are breaking away from their past. Drawing up a single reform program for all of these countries, which have different histories, conditions, and traditions, is futile. Each socialist country must find its own solutions to its own problems.

At the same time, such principles as democracy, regard for human rights and liberties, promotion of universal human values, establishment of a self-regulating economy, and respect for the moral and cultural values of each people will dominate the activities of the public forces, which are playing a key role in the present situation in the Soviet Union and the other socialist countries. I don't think that Socialism has lost its appeal.

What is your assessment about the future of Socialism in Eastern Europe?

Today the socialist countries are in a state of turmoil. Alongside honest citizens wanting life in their countries to change for the better are dishonest and self-serving individuals seeking to further their own political ambitions. But intolerance justified by the desire to solve all problems at once can lead to new, bitter disappointments. The political struggle in my country bears this out.

A break with the past is always dramatic, and sometimes tragic. People who have committed crimes must be punished. Public anger against those who so solemnly held the public trust for years is justified. But it is dangerous for society to waste people's energy on revenge.

Among the members of these parties of the countries of Eastern Europe are courageous and honest people - people who awakened the public by their ideas and actions. It isn't fair to paint these people with the same brush as the bankrupt political leaders from the upper echelons of power.

Only a society in which constructive elements prevail and in which common sense and justice govern public actions is capable of making progress.

The past year has seen many historic changes across a familiar landscape. Do you believe the immediate future is likely to erupt in violence and chaos?

I am convinced that 1990 will be a tumultuous year for the Soviet Union and for our friends and allies in the Warsaw Treaty countries and the Council for Mutual Economic Assistance. We are in for many surprises, including unpleasant ones. Yet, I am sure that further movement toward democracy and progress based on human rights and dignity will be easier if our countries succeed in establishing more balanced, diverse, and meaningful relations among them. We have already begun to restructure our relations in keeping with the new realities, based on full respect for the right of every people to decide its own destiny. Free choice is best, and cooperation is the most constructive way to implement this choice.

SOCIALISM TOMORROW

Where is it headed?

Poland, Hungary, the German Democratic Republic, Bulgaria, Czechoslovakia, and Romania have entered into a period of radical reforms. It is noted everywhere that the Soviet Union not only hailed and supported the revolutionary changes happening in the Warsaw Treaty countries, but also encouraged them by its policy of Perestroika and its unconditional denunciation of the Stalinist model of socialism.

It is more or less clear what the Eastern European countries want to break with. They have said No to the administrative-command system and the one-party monopoly on power. They have said No to ideological dogmatism and the system of power that ignore the fundamental laws of economic and political development. They have said No to dishonest, corrupt, and immoral leaders who usurped the right to declare what was right and what was wrong on behalf of the party and the people. They have said No to many things, so I repeat, this is more or less clear.

Other questions are far more difficult to answer: Where are the Eastern European countries heading? How will their social systems develop? What factors will dominate the development of what has recently been referred to as the "socialist community" and the "nucleus of the world socialist system"?

Answers to these questions are coming both from people who are directly involved in the stormy process of renewal and from sideline spectators who are watching the swift change of characters and events.

In a nutshell, the points of view fall into several categories: First, socialism has suffered a defeat. Communist ideology is dead. The only possible future is a return to the bourgeois-democratic system. In other words, onward to the past.

Second, that a long overdue shift has finally occurred. In the international dispute between the Communists and the Social-Democrats, who were so zealously and ardently condemned and discredited during Stalin's time, the Social-Democrats have won. That is why, they say, social-democratic methods should be used to cure the ills of the Eastern European countries.

Third, the revolutionary changes in Eastern Europe will cleanse the socialist ideal and rid it of the tragic follies of Stalinist-style Socialism. Newly found freedom will enable Eastern Europeans to make a quick recovery, to discard false values, and to embrace the true values of socialism.

All these points of view have a right to exist, but I don't think it's correct to attempt to map out a single course for all of the socialist countries that are breaking away from their past. Drawing up a single reform program for all of these countries, which have different histories, conditions, and traditions, is futile. Each socialist country must find its own solutions to its own problems.

At the same time, such principles as democracy, regard for human rights and liberties, promotion of universal human values, establishment of a self-regulating economy, and respect for the moral and cultural values of each people will dominate the activities of the public forces, which are playing a key role in the present situation in the Soviet Union and the other socialist countries. I don't think that socialism has lost its appeal, but it has certainly lost most of its credibility.

Today the socialist countries are in a state of turmoil. Alongside honest citizens wanting life in their countries to change for the better are dishonest and self-serving individuals seeking to further their own political ambitions. But intolerance justified by the desire to solve all problems at once can lead to new, bitter disappointments. The political struggle in my country bears this out.

A break with the past is always dramatic, and sometimes tragic. People who have committed crimes must be punished. Public anger against those who so solemnly held the public trust for years is justified. But it is dangerous for society to waste people's energy on revenge.

Among the members of these parties of the countries of Eastern Europe are courageous and honest people - people who awakened the public by their ideas and actions. It isn't fair to paint these people with the same brush as the bankrupt political leaders from the upper echelons of power. Only a society in which constructive elements prevail and in which common sense and justice govern public actions is capable of making progress.

I am convinced that 1990 will be a tumultuous year for the Soviet Union and for our friends and allies in the Warsaw Treaty countries and the Council for Mutual Economic Assistance. We are in for many surprises, including unpleasant ones. Yet, I am sure that further movement toward democracy and progress based on human rights and dignity will be easier if our countries succeed in establishing more balanced, diverse, and meaningful relations among them.

We have already begun to restructure our relations in keeping with the new realities, based on full respect for the right of every people to decide its own destiny. Free choice is best, and cooperation is the most constructive way to implement this choice.

HISTORY AS LIES

Blank Spots in Soviet History Slowly Filling In

We in the West have always adopted a self-righteous attitude vis-a-vis the Soviets. We convinced ourselves that our form of government was superior to theirs. We assured ourselves that the freedoms enjoyed were real and substantial compared to the artificial freedoms espoused in the Constitution of the U.S.S.R. And we confidently promoted our way of life, and our world view to billions of people in every nation on earth to the exclusion of the Communists.

The surprising thing is that the people of the Soviet Union, led by the Party and its massive propaganda machinery, resolutely embraced a remarkably similar attitude. Theirs, not our form of government, was the highest idea of mankind. Their freedoms, the rights to employment, health care, inexpensive housing, to be free of profligate economics, etc., were eminently more important than any rights Americans supposedly enjoyed. They could promote this view with the conviction they were "Building the Road to Communism" for all mankind.

Facts are facts. No one can say who was right and who was wrong. In the long gray field that is our world, certainty is a luxury the ground will not yield. Yet of all the philosophical knots created over the course of the Cold War, no facts are more certain than the systematic methods the Soviets utilized to change and distort historical truths. Soviet history, especially recent history, had become so riddled with lies that it became laughable to outsiders. Sadly, however, the lies were almost universally believed by the masses commanded by the omnipotent Communist Party.

This state of affairs created many outrageous incidents as truth collided with fabrication. In 1949, a mid-level U.S. State Department envoy, on a secret mission to Moscow just prior to the detonation of the "Red Bomb," was forced to cancel his prepared remarks at a foreign relations conference when his Russian handlers discovered he intended to quantify the amounts of food and medical supplies the U.S. had supplied the Soviet Union during the late war. The Soviet people it seems, had learned that their heroic resistance to Nazism was a long and lonely fight, and the British and Americans paid but lip service to their promises of aid.

In another strange but true tale, *The Great Soviet Encyclopedia* was amended following the execution of former NKVD Chief Lavrenty Beria in 1953. Subscribers around the world, including most university libraries, were sent a new and expanded entry on the Barents Sea to replace the biographical sketch of Beria. Though the mailing contained detailed instructions on how to cut and remove the appropriate pages, it lacked even the most rudimentary explanation of its purpose. It's probably safe to say they couldn't imagine anyone possibly questioning or objecting to their "editorial discretion".

Then in 1956, when Khrushchev read his secret speech to the 20th Party Congress (and carefully selected guests), history again took a twist. Stalin, who for more than thirty years had been defied as the "Titan of Soviet Thought" and the "Greatest Leader the World Had Ever Known," among hundreds of other bombastic accolades, was vilified as a demonic dictator, a mass murderer and the author of everything wrong about the Party and the Nation. Virtually over-night, statues and busts of Stalin were removed from all public places, cities named in his honor were renamed and his reputation was flushed down the proverbial toilet of history. Truth once again clashed with reality. Millions of Soviet citizens, having taken their marching orders from the Party hierarchy, changed their innermost beliefs with hardly a breath. "If the Party says Stalin was a villain then that's just what he was!" Allegiance to the Soviet Truth was automatic.

Imagine then, the shock and disappointment they must have experienced as all of their truths had become shattered just as quickly. The Communist Party, the "eternal vanguard of progressive humanity," was now admitting it seriously erred in all aspects of its policies. The nation was not the beacon of peace and freedom it described itself as, but was instead an instigator of war and oppression. The Soviet economy, far from being the "Dazzling Child of Marxist-Leninist Triumph," was a shattered core of broken-down industries and inefficient agricultural collectives. To an ideologically-driven society, it was a cruel confession indeed.

How do people react to such an awakening? The story is an interesting one.

Events of fifty and sixty years ago are now discussed as if they happened only yesterday. It's as if a ghostly vacuum of time withdrew to its mysterious realm, lighting previously darkened places like a match in a cellar. Indeed, the very word Glasnost, the moniker under which the current reappraisal of the past is being conducted, literally means "opening a long closed thing." It's a fitting label for such an undertaking, for many long closed things are now coming open; the blank spots in Soviet history are becoming filled in.

One telling example is the truth of the so-called Molotov-Von Ribbentrop Pact of 1939, recently repudiated by the Supreme Soviet as an illegal treaty which made the onset of The Second World War inevitable. To the West, the pact was a dastardly deed designed to satiate both Hitler's and Stalin's designs on the Baltic republics (Estonia, Lithuania and Latvia), Poland and Romania. To the Soviets, however, it was a practical and expedient agreement forced upon them by the Germans and justified by gaining them time to build their armed forces. While to objectivists it may have been both, whatever it was, the Soviet government consistently refused to acknowledge the pact even existed after the war. All references to it were wiped out of accounts of the war and history books that had been published since. It was, as one western historian described, "but one of the many non-events of Soviet diplomacy."

It was no wonder then that Novosti's London Bureau Chief Vladimir Dobkin, in 1978, was forced to eat his words when he wrote in the London Times that his country did all it could to prevent World War II from erupting. The incredulous Soviet journalist stood in disbelief as his essay was roundly ostracized in the British press. What had he written that was so inflammatory to his allies in the War? He was actually stumped.

Only years later did Dobkin learn the reason for his mistreatment. He, like all Soviet citizens, learned that his nation, under the watchful eyes of the beloved Stalin, warned the stubborn West that Hitler was a madman, intent on conquering all of Europe and much of the rest of the world. He had no cause to dispute this lesson and little, if any, reference to question it. He was, despite his presence in the West, a captive of the collective mind think the Party instilled in the masses. Unfortunately, it was based upon a mountain of lies. So potent is the truth, that the fearless Communist dictatorship was forced to hide it.

Other, more private incidents also stand out. On a visit to Smolensk in 1987, I and a colleague had the pleasure of addressing a group of about two hundred university students at a cultural exchange program. When my friend responded to a question about a remark he made concerning the brutal conduct of Soviet forces in Afghanistan, the students started laughing at his description of a village massacre. We couldn't understand what was so funny, dismissing their reaction to a translator's play of the language. Only later did we learn that the students laughed in disbelief. They had always been told that the Soviet army was invited into Afghanistan to help the friendly government in Kabul combat a group of Western-backed mercenary guerillas who routinely murdered innocents and destroyed public facilities in an effort to destabilize a nation sharing a border with the U.S.S.R. It was unthinkable that Soviet soldiers did anything other than save children and render medical care to defenseless villagers. As it turned out, they might have just as well laughed at themselves for being so soundly fooled.

That same day I had a serious row with a pretty student named Marina. Her delicate looks and shy demeanor shielded a steadfast, almost egotistical reliance on the Communist Party and Soviet government. We were discussing Soviet citizenship practices and how they related to political dissidents. To Marina, dissent simply did not exist in the U.S.S.R. Everyone supported the Party not because they were forced to, but because they agreed with its every move. This belief fostered the notion that independent-minded people were political extremists, who were in turn mentally ill and, thus, could not be shut away in state hospitals with impunity.

"Then why," I asked, "does your country strip people of their citizenship and then exile them abroad?"

"We don't!" insisted Marina. "Anybody who leaves does so as a result of free choice."

"Then why aren't they allowed to return?" I asked.

"They are," she said. "In fact they frequently do," she added.

Knowing she was referring to the celebrated few examples of Russians who came home after "alienating sojourns" in the West, and whose cases were funneled through the propaganda mills to emerge as unassailable proof that Communism was superior to Capitalism, I countered:

"But what about all the defectors, the best and brightest of your arts and sporting community? Why are they not permitted to return?"

"Because they have succumbed to the glamour of bourgeois materialism and have forfeited their right to be reunited with their Soviet brethren," she responded.

"Then you admit they cannot return?"

"Nothing of the kind," she said. "They can, but we don't want them anymore."

After about ten minutes more of such banter, a conversation that I admit reminded me more a children's game than an adult conversation, I realized that further discussion was useless. I was fairly confident of the facts as I understood them. She was convinced otherwise and had the added advantage of knowing the specifics of Soviet law.

Fortunately, I stayed in contact with Marina. Each subsequent letter I received from her showed a characteristically gentle, but ever so slight adjustment in her views. She finally admitted my point that Soviet practice diverged dramatically with Soviet law. Thereafter, she seemed to chuck her previous feelings altogether. She even went so far as to propose marriage to me in an effort to get out of the rapidly disintegrating Soviet Union.

It is I who has the last laugh. But I'm not laughing. Instead I'm thinking about all of those brave men and women who perished after first being dubbed *Enemies of the People*.

Part II
PEOPLE

GORBY, WE HARDLY KNEW YA'

His Storybook Rise to the Top of the Party

Mikhail Sergeyevich Gorbachev. Born March 2, 1931 in the town of Privol'noye, Krasnogvardeisk District of the Stavropolsky Territory, Russian Federated Republic, U.S.S.R. After holding a variety of Party and government posts, he was elected General Secretary of the Central Committee of the Communist Party of the Soviet Union on March 12, 1985.

That much we know. We also know that this fellow from the steppes is the owner and creator of a peculiar brand of frenzy that is sweeping the West, *Gorby Fever*. But apart from the news and headlines, what do we really know about the man who sits in the highest chair in the Kremlin? That's a good question. You better believe it's on the minds of every intelligence chief west of the Elbe.

In analyzing the career of any official in the Soviet Union it is important to keep in mind that no one rises within the state apparatus without simultaneously rising within the Party hierarchy. These two institutions of Soviet power, while operationally separate, are actually so completely intermingled by personnel and prerogatives that the lines between them become a great blur of grey.

Growing up in a rural community over-populated by simple peasant families didn't suit young Mikhail. But the destruction caused by the war curtailed his wanderlust. As food was in a great demand, regulations issued by Stalin prohibited people from leaving collective farms without permission. Owing to a good harvest in 1949, he and his fellow combine operators from Privol'noye were awarded the prestigious Order of the Red Banner. Already a member of the Komsomol Communist Youth League, he applied for his party card at age 18 and received it about three years later, according to strict probationary rules. Mikhail must have been very proud. His family must have been very impressed. Little did they know this was but the first wrung of a very high ladder which he would rapidly climb.

In 1950 he applied for and was accepted into the law program at Moscow State University. For a country boy, this was some feat. Founded in 1755 by the distinguished writer, poet and educator Mikhail K. Lomonosov, whose namesake the school still officially bears, Moscow State University is the premier institution for higher learning in the country.

Upon his graduation Gorbachev conveniently avoided a position in the procurator's office, which by that time was busily re-evaluating cases of the repression by Stalin, Beria and their henchmen. Instead, he applied for and received the appointed post of department head in his former territorial Komsomol in Stavropol. It was not a particularly good job, but for a man who planned on making a career in the Party, it was a heck of a good start.

He must have impressed his elders. A year later in 1956 he was promoted to the position of First Secretary of the Stavropol Komsomol City Committee. For the following two years it was his job to groom the local youth and recruit them for service in the youth league. It's the kind of job where you can make good friends, and enemies. Another promotion came his way in late 1958. Now the 37-year old Gorbachev became the Second and then First Party Secretary for the Komsomol for the entire territorial committee. It was a big promotion!

But bigger things were to come. In 1962 Gorbachev was kicked up the proverbial stairs. He became, in succession: Department Chief of the territorial committee of the Party; First Secretary of the city-committee; Second Secretary of the territorial committee and finally, in 1970, First Secretary of the Stavropolsky CPSU Territorial Committee.

It was in this position and as a member of the all-important Central Committee that Gorbachev earned a name for himself. Having graduated with his Master's Degree from the Stavropol Agriculture Institute in 1967, Gorbachev led his territory in the area or agrarian economics to such a degree that he was awarded a kind of "man of the year" award, called a Schtotya, from his bosses in the Smolensk Regional CPSU Executive Committee. The Stavropolsky Kray (Territory) is a Constituent member of the Smolensk Oblast (Region), a semi-autonomous part of the Russian Republic.

As Stavropol party boss he frequently travelled to Moscow and entertained higher Party officials at Krasnye Kamni, a sanitarium for the Moscow elite near the Stavropolsky town of Kislovodsk. Fortunately for him, this town just happened to be the locale of KGB chief Yuri Andropov's government dacha.

Over the next several years their friendship flourished. The anxious Gorbachev jumped on Andropov's bandwagon just as it was headed for the Party Secretariat. By a series of cruel but spectacular moves, the truth of which has largely been confirmed by Glasnost-speaking officials, Andropov skillfully engineered himself to become Leonid Brezhnev's only possible successor.

That Gorbachev played a role in these affairs, which included murder, blackmail and treachery of the highest villainy, there can be no doubt. Not only did he oblige his mentor by denouncing Brezhnev cohorts, he also sided with the KGB and Red Army in agreeing to send troops into Afghanistan. As we now know, that decision was another surprise in Andropov's bag of tricks to discredit Brezhnev. It was a disaster, of course, but then Solidarity-plagued Poland came along and Brezhnev's ineptitude became clear. Andropov left the KGB to his well-groomed deputy and took a seat as Central Committee Secretary, second in seniority only to "Old Eyebrows" himself.

He brought along Gorbachev directly thereafter and promoted him to Party Secretary in charge of national agriculture policy. At last, Gorbachev made the big move to Moscow, an absolutely vital move for anybody seeking a seat in the Politburo, the country's and Party's highest executive body.

\Gorbachev readily backed Andropov against the so-called "Dnepropetrovsk Mafia" in the Politburo. This group of geriatrics consisted of Brezhnev, Prime Minister Nikolai Tikhonov, and Central Committee Secretaries Andrei Kirilenko and Konstantin Chernenko. Though they were too powerful for Andropov to touch directly, they were left bare by the likes of Gorbachev, Grigori Romonov (Leningrad Party chief) and Geider Aliyev (Armenia's Party chief and Premier), who executed Andropov's orders to ruin the careers of all of the old-timers' protégés. There's no telling how many careers were destroyed by their intrigues. Each man was handsomely rewarded with a Politburo seat.

Gorbachev also stood firmly behind Andropov's anti-corruption and anti-alcohol campaigns. With fierce loyalty and devotion, he toured the nation preaching the virtues of discipline and hard work. For a comparative youngster (age 49) Gorbachev enjoyed a substantial amount of power; all thanks to Andropov, the ruthless leader of the KGB.

Most of us know the story after that. When Andropov died, rather than rocking the boat, Gorbachev politely nominated Chernenko to the top Party post. But he knew his time would come. And it did, perhaps sooner than he had planned. As we have seen, Gorbachev had his own ideas.

In the United States, Britain and West Germany politicians have been quick to praise him. Even Ronald Reagan has been seduced by the twin notions of Glasnost and Perestroika. In fact, his warm embrace of Gorbachev is such that it has angered a good many of his staunchest conservative supporters. "Yes, he's different enough," they warn, "but he's also the same character that covered up Chernobyl. He's personally responsible for the arrest of American journalist Nick Danilov on trumped-up spy charges. His tis-for-tat policy regarding embassy personnel expulsions is responsible for removal of at least 87 western diplomats from Moscow."

The fact that he rose so quickly and so high within the Party proves he is capable and clever. His quick grab for power in the following two years was nothing short of spectacular. Not only did he wrestle the Central Committee in his favor, but he also succeeded in removing any potential opponent from the Politburo. Gone were Romanov, Aliyev, Tikhonov, and three other old guard members. It's safe to presume that each replacement member owes his political soul to Gorbachev.

With the police and the military on his side, who can guess what's next? If the past is any guide, the purging will continue until the entire national, republic and regional party apparatus are firmly under his control. Expect bombshells at the upcoming Party Plenum meeting in Moscow scheduled for next month. It's a sure bet.

As we in the West watch and wait, a remark of Andrei Gromyko's comes to mind at the Central Committee meeting which elected him General Secretary. Gromyko reportedly said, "Can you trust him gentlemen? He has a nice smile it's true, but his teeth are made of steel."

That's not only a good quote in this world of danger, that's a good lesson too.

THE MYSTIC OF MOSCOW

Alan Chumak and Others Mesmerize Masses

MOSCOW: His face is friendly and round. His complexion is clear and pink as a suckling pig. Were it not for his curly gray hair he might be viewed as a giant infant. But the power of his stare is mesmerizing millions of Soviet citizens.

His name is Alan Chumak and he is the resident TV psychic of the popular morning program 120 Minutes. For the past seven months his daily "sessions" have administered a mysterious healing to television viewers from Armenia to Vladivostok. Through a combination of mystical gestures, meditation and glaring straight into the television camera, Chumak claims to have cured scores of terminally ill, retarded and suffering people through the magic of the airwaves.

However, don't take his word for it. Ask any one of the thousands of Soviets who attest to his curative powers. In fact, he's become so popular that his apartment manager has threatened to evict him because of the daily throng that gathers outside his building waiting for the chance to be personally healed by him. When conservative-minded officials, alarmed by the size Chumak's following, ordered him off-the-air, a thunderstorm of protest resulted. Chumak was back on television after only one week.

And he is not the only one. Mystics, seers, healers and psychics are now commonly featured on both national and local television programs. It has become, the words of one Soviet TV executive from Volgograd, "a disturbing phenomenon the likes of which is unparalleled."

"Soviet television is not known for its innovations," said Alexander Bogdonov, "but I think this has gone too far." He estimates that between 25-40 million viewers now regularly watch their favorite TV gurus. Not all of them seek to heal, however. Others teach meditation, astrology, relaxation techniques, stress relief and psychic recall. Collectively they are ushering into light the long darkened truth about mysticism and parapsychology practices in modern Soviet society. Having formally shunned religion and other "mystical faiths and beliefs" for the past 72 years, the sudden rise in popularity of Chumak's brand of mysticism has become an unexpected by-product of President Mikhail Gorbachev's process of change and renewal.

"The Russian people have always been superstitious," explained Bogdonov. "This was a consequence of the sudden discouragement in the official religion directly after the revolution in 1917. The people's interest in spiritual practices was already awakened due to the ritualistic nature of the Russian Orthodox faith."

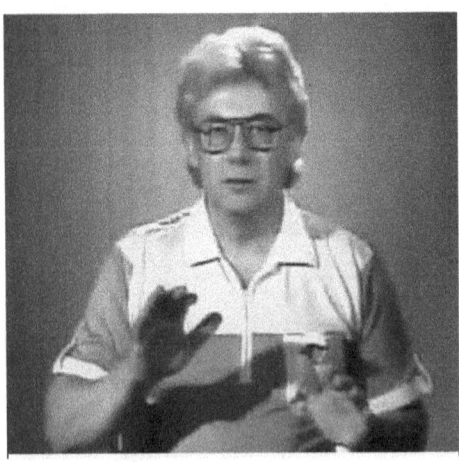

Healer Alan Cumak on television: : I treat the soul Photo by Victor Reznikov. Reprinted courtesy of Soviet Life.

In an interview he recently gave to the *Moscow News*, Chumak said he knew nothing of his psychic powers until, as a television correspondent, he was sent to report on an old man with extrasensory perception (ESP). "I was a skeptic and did not believe that such things could really be true," he said. "But after speaking with this man, I started to look at the world in a different way. It turned out that I had always had certain qualities which many people regard as mystic. I started developing them and learned to use my gift to heal people."

Chumak's methods are as mysterious as his powers. After warming up his viewers with soothing talk, he asks them to remain still while he transmits himself into a state of deep concentration. Following a period of time which may last from several seconds to ten minutes or more, his closed eyes open slowly. A piercing glare quickly emerges. Then, after another uncertain interval, he begins to waive his hands and arms with magical movements.

This process, according to Chumak, permits him to absorb people's ills and sufferings into his own body. He then imagines himself well, which correspondingly heals the viewers too. The secret, he says, is in wanting to be healed.

"I can't describe the reason scientifically. All I know is what I feel and what the people tell me," he said. "I am sure, however, that those who have become healed are deeply faithful people. It is the energy which flows between us."

Chumak prefers to appear on TV because "it is the most convenient way to heal a large audience." But he is quick to add, "I didn't find TV. They found me." The decision to put him on television was made in response to the oft-unruly crowds that attended his public sessions.

His supporters eagerly tout his curative powers. Andrei Chistov, a retiree from Moscow, had suffered low back pain for three years. After watching a series of Chumak's morning sessions, he said the felling returned to his legs. "And the inflammation went down and I can walk without pain," he said.

In case one was not lucky enough to see Chumak in person or on television, he tells sufferers not to worry. The mystic instructs them to leave the television set on and place a jar of oil or cream in front of it. His magical gestures act as a "charging agent" on the liquid, which the person can then use to heal himself of any ailment from aching muscles to heart disease.

Chumak's eventual goal is to establish an institute and fund medical centers for the terminally ill around the Soviet Union. He believes that most people contain powers like his and he hopes to develop a method for teaching it to others. Members of the Soviet elite have also been known to schedule appointments with Chumak. In characteristic perestroika form he said they have to stand in line like everybody else.

Soviet Psychic Killed Trying to Stop Oncoming Train

Yevgeny Frankel was one of the Soviet Union's growing number of psychic healers and mentalists. He claimed he could use his powers to stop bicycles, automobiles and street cars. Last September, he thought he was ready for something bigger, so he stopped in front of a freight train. Unfortunately, his alleged powers failed him and he was instantly killed.

The train's engineer said to the press that Frankel stepped onto the tracks with his arms raised, head lowered and body tensed. The daily newspaper Sovietskaya Rossiya reported investigators looking for clues to Frankel's decision found an explanation in a briefcase he left on the platform in the southern city of Astrakhan.

"First I stopped a bicycle, then cars and then a streetcar," wrote the deceased. "Now I am going to stop a speeding train."

A police captain speculated that Frankel's belief in his own power was so strong that he felt stopping a train would be the ultimate test.

It would certainly have added to his celebrity, he added. Frankel was popular on Astrakhan television. An estimated six thousand mourners attended his funeral. The newspaper report failed to mention any survivors.

Mentalist Evgeny Frankel claims to be able to stop cars and trains by force of his concentration and will power. He will never get another chance to prove his powers.
Photo courtesy of SovietskayaRossiya

*Though official numbers were never released, it is believed that upwards of 300 people were trampled to death during the fervor of Stalin's funeral procession
Reprinted courtesy of Sputnik*

WHERE WERE YOU WHEN STALIN DIED?

A Moment Frozen in Time

Soviet citizens in their forties and older remember exactly where they were and what they were doing on March 6, 1953, the day it was announced that Josef Stalin had died. It's a phenomenon stronger but not unlike Americans' recollection of the same things when President John Kennedy was assassinated ten and a half years later.

How could they forget, Stalin was a living god. He was at once their master and their servant; their protector of their freedom and the defender of the territory. To the average Russian who suffered through poverty, revolution, civil war, two massive armed invasions and a perceived world conspiracy to encircle the Soviet Union, these were important attributes. Stalin was all-knowing and all-seeing. Through all the tumult, Stalin stood as a symbol of unity and stability. It didn't matter that he had a tough side, he never let it show.

His sudden death, (some believe he was murdered by his Kremlin colleagues for fear of a bloody new purge) sent ordinary citizens into a panic. Would the Americans use the occasion to launch a nuclear strike against the Soviet Union? Could anyone fill his enormous shoes? Though official figures have never been released, it has been estimated that more than two hundred people were trampled to death during his gigantic funeral. Still others committed suicide rather than face life without the security Stalin supposedly guaranteed.

The following are actual statements from the several dozen interviews in which I asked the simple question, "Where were you when Stalin died?"

I was on a construction site. Suddenly somber music came over the loud speakers. After two hours the director announced the leader's death. None of us knew what to do—so, of course, we all went and got smashed."

Bulat Akedzian, stonemason
Yerevan

"We received the body with dignity. I immediately thought about my dear friend Sasha, who played Stalin on stage and screen. The resemblance was amazing. If Stalin's corpse would not take to the embalming chemicals, Sasha's life would be in great danger?"

Nicolai Voronov, pathologist,
Moscow

"We were in class at school. The principal rang the alarm which meant we had to line up outside. She was obviously moved because she stood there shaking for five minutes before she broke the news. My first reaction was to laugh. Seeing your teachers bawling like babies is funny to a 7-year-old."

Yuri Ivanov, photographer,
Saratov

"I was in bed when the phone rang. It was the boss and his voice was filled with panic. He and other bigwigs were with the body to make sure it didn't move. Many said Stalin would stage his own death to find out who was disloyal. Then the doctors arrived and it was official. We didn't know whether to be happy or sad. For this reason we mostly stayed home and listened to the radio."

Alexei Ostenpenko, Yeltsin aide,
Kiev

"I was driving this very bus. Suddenly all the traffic stopped. The militia swarmed onto the streets and started yanking people from their vehicles. We were ordered to stand in silence. When I asked an officer what was happening he told me to shut up and obey the order. There we were, thousands standing in the streets without an inkling why. Nobody really believed the leader would die."

Tarek Mitishevelli, bus driver,
Tiblisi

"I was standing in line for butter and cheese. The news came whispering down the column of people. Many fainted, others wept and beat themselves. I was struck with fear of the future. Would I ever taste sweet butter again?"

Anna Stakanova, seamstress,
Odessa

t was cold outside but they made us march into the schoolyard and sing songs praising Stalin. I don't believe any of us resented having to do it because we saw how visibly shaken our teachers were. I probably felt something bad was going to happen to us now. Then one kid started crying, and then a second. I don't know if it was real sorrowful crying or fake crying for show. Pretty soon we were all crying like a mob, balling our eyes out for what seemed like hours. Then it was suddenly over and we went back to our classrooms and continued our lessons.

Simeon Kirilov, construction engineer,
Moscow

I was working on a pipeline construction project. I and a few other men were in a deep ditch, covered in mud. We were ordered out of the ditch and made to stand at attention as we sang a tribute to Stalin which was popular during The Great Patriotic War. I felt rather silly because we were all so filthy but it didn't seem to matter to anybody else. A few of us started crying and others were embracing and kissing everyone around them. After about thirty minutes, we didn't know what to do so we went back into our hole and continued digging. A few minutes later, our foreman screamed at us and said we were being disrespectful. So, we all went home and took the next three days off.

Boris Zarenko, pipefitter
Orel

All I can remember, I saw people crying, everywhere. I was young and the cause for their sadness was a mystery to me. Only afterward did I learn it was due to Stalin's death. So, I started crying too because it would look bad if I didn't.

Sofia Harbin. Seamstress
Moscow

I was at my office job as a book-keeper in the district Soviet of Brest. My only thought was "What is going to happen now?" I think everyone felt the same way. We continued working because we didn't know what else to do. When solemn music came on the radio station, we all stood up and bowed our heads. It seemed like we stood there forever.

Marko Tinarenko, accountant
Minsk

It was a rainy, gray day in Murmansk. Very cold too. I was at home and I heard a lot of commotion in the hallway of my apartment building. I opened the door to see what was going on and I saw people scurrying up and down the hall not knowing what to do or where to go. I went back inside and looked out the window. Our apartment was on the tenth floor of the building and I could see people running around in every direction. I didn't know what to do so I went back inside and waited until things calmed down. That didn't happen until at least the following day. Everyone was expected to line up outside in the bleak weather while loud speakers played patriotic songs. My wife and I joined in and started crying because everyone else was crying too.

Stephan Boronik, school teacher
Moscow

I remember loud explosions and we all went outside to see what was going on. It was a military unit shooting off cannons in tribute to the leader. All the work places were closed and everyone was supposed to go to their local party headquarters to offer condolences to each other. There was a book that each of us had to sign to prove we were there. I remember feeling

sorry for those who didn't come. I was afraid they might get in trouble for not mourning him.

ArtanDarakjian, factory watchman
Yerevan, Armenia

There was nobody to tell us what to do so we weren't sure what we should be doing or where we should go. Later that night, we were told to assemble in the central square and pay our respects by singing songs to Stalin's memory. I remember a lot of people crying; others where just silent and bowed their heads. I felt that I needed to show my sadness so I wore a black arm band and pretty soon everybody else was wearing one too. Mine was made out of a black rag I found in a trash heap behind the big building. I was hoping nobody saw me because it might be misconstrued as a disrespectful act. Thankfully, nobody did.

Anton Polyansky, theater manager
Tallin, Estonia

I was at our university library and an announcement came over the speakers. It instructed us to go outside and assemble in the courtyard, which all of us did. We didn't know what was going on. Then people started to whisper that Stalin was ill. The idea that he was dead never entered our minds.

Irina Derakovna, university lecturer
Volgograd

I was in secondary school. We were told to go outside and line up in front of the building to hear an address from our principal. I can't recall what he said but I could see he was really chocked up. And so too were all our teachers and the administrators. Then somebody started wailing and pretty soon everybody started crying and lost their composure. I started too because it seemed like the right thing to do.

Bitar Marie Saratsovna, university librarian
Riga, Latvia

USSR Foreign Minister Vyacheslav Mikhailovich Molotov (center wearing glasses) with Nazi Foreign Minister Joachim von Ribbentrop (at left) pictured at the signing ceremony of the Soviet-German Non-agression Pact in August 1939. A secret protocol envisioned the partition of Poland and the end of independence for the three Baltic republics Estonia, Lithuania and Latvia. For the following forty years, the Soviets refused to admit the pact exists and this and other photos were "blanked-out" of Soviet history books and encyclopedias, etc. This form of censorship was consistently used to cancel unpleasant truths and eliminate notable people from the written record. After being deposed by Khrushchev in 1957 as a leader of the s-called "Anti-Party Bloc," Molotov's name and image was similarly blotted out.

MOLOTOV: THE LAST OF THE LAMBS

From Stalin's Side to Seclusion and Obscurity

The announcement from the Council of Ministers was terse. "After a lengthy and grave illness, V.M. Molotov has died in a Moscow hospital. He was 96."

And that was it.

The exact cause of his death, and its date was not revealed. The fact that the news was released on November 8, 1987, a day after the 69th Anniversary of the Great October Revolution, suggests that he may have died very much earlier. The Soviets are sharp cookies. They wouldn't want a name like Molotov, or should I say "Molotov's ghost," interfering with their festivities.

Just who was this Molotov you ask?

Let me tell you. Vyacheslav Mikhailovich Molotov was born in wilds of northern Russia in 1890. He was reported to be an exceptionally bright student, but by age 5 he joined in the 1905 rebellion against the tsar. After that he became a devoted Marxist and was one of the founding fathers of the Communist Party's daily organ. Pravda. When the Bolsheviks finally seized control of the fledgling Russian parliament, the Duma, he was seated with Lenin at the helm of Soviet power.

After Lenin's death in 1924, Molotov wisely chose to ally himself with Joseph Stalin. From 1930-1941 Molotov was the Soviet Premier. As such he was in direct control of the heavy industrialization and forced collectivization that transformed the weak and backward Russian sprawl into a major economic power. In 1939, having been favored by Stalin with the additional title of foreign minister, Molotov negotiated and signed the infamous Soviet-German Nonaggression Pact. For those of you who know your history, that agreement made World War II inevitable. It started less than a week later.

During the war Molotov was named Chief Liaison to Allied Forces. It was his job to soak up as much Lend-Lease aid from the U.S. as he could. We all know that he did a great job. In terms of sheer tonnage, the Soviet Union got six times more equipment, supplies and ammunition than all of our other allies put together. After the war, Molotov, being always a Party man, was forced to denounce his wife as "an agent of provocation and cosmopolitanism." She was imprisoned and died there. He remained a member of the Politburo.

When Khrushchev succeeded Stalin, Molotov made the mistake of throwing his support behind Georgi Malenkov, Stalin's appointed successor. This was his first big mistake. In June, 1957 he was dismissed from his seat on the all-powerful Central Committee for siding with the so-called "anti-Party group". He was posted as the U.S.S.R. ambassador to Mongolia. It was a meteoric fall from power, the likes of which only seem possible under Communist regimes.

In 1962, Khrushchev finally succeeded in getting Malenkov, Molotov and others expelled from the Party. All the towns, parks and streets bearing their names were changed, literally overnight. Molotov became an official nobody. In recognition of their bloody deeds, Molotov and others were castigated as "Stalin's lambs." Yet here was a man who stood at the very center of the first 40 years of Soviet rule. He participated in the revolution, civil war, the purges, the mass terror and the complete subjugation of the Soviet people to the Party and the police.

He was the man who involuntarily gave his name to the Molotov cocktail, that Finnish creation of the 1930's which consisted of a gasoline-filled bottle with a rag stuffed fuse. It was against the Red Army that they were first thrown. He was the man who surely countersigned all of Stalin's death orders and probably orchestrated the shameful show trials of 1937-1940. Make no mistake about it, Molotov was a killer!

He didn't look like one, however, Molotov was a small man with a square head and a bristly moustache. His neat appearance and bookish style would have better fit a small-town librarian. Yet he was a master organizer and administrator. When Stalin wanted something done, he would order Molotov to do it. Many stories are still told of how Stalin abused and berated Molotov in public. But this apparently never bothered the little man. He would have called it "Party discipline."

It is the study of characters such as Molotov that so enriched the art and science of Kremlinology. I'm sure I'm not alone in saying, "Something went out of the world the day Molotov died". The fascinating and contradictory personalities who stalked the secret halls of the Kremlin are now all gone. While the present Soviet leadership must be breathing a collective sigh of relief, Kremlinologists in the West are ruling the day. "Think of all the secrets that many knew? Did he write his memoirs?" If he did, we'll probably never get the chance to read them. Glasnost notwithstanding, the Soviets still have a lot about the past they'd just as well keep hidden. Thus, Molotov remained a Party man to the end. The consummate apparatchik became a consummate nobody, just the way his successors wanted.

Still, Molotov must have felt bitter about it all. His pain surely was aided by the news that Konstantin Chernenko succeeded in getting Molotov his party membership card back in 1984. Though he was not officially rehabilitated, he was at least permitted to send his maid to the Kremlin's gastronomy.

Few are the rewards, he must have thought, for being labeled by Lenin in 1917, "The best filing clerk in Russia."

AGAINST THE GRAIN

BORIS YELTSIN
An Autobiography

BORIS THE BOLD

Yeltsin Autobiography an Informative Puff Job

It was October 1988 and I was in Moscow. On a cold, rainy evening my friend Eugene Sykov, who was an editor for Novosti Press Agency, was taking me on a tour of the city's impressive subway system. We rode the trains aimlessly, visited about a dozen clean and ornate stations, and all the while Eugene explained the membership dues rules of the Communist Party to me. On our way back to the Komsomolskaya Station, which is adjacent to the Foreign Ministry building in Moscow's northwest quadrant, four men were making their way through the train. They were Boris Yeltsin, his brother-in-law and two aides. I was told they were auditing the system. When we were introduced Yeltsin was eager to hear an American's opinion of the subway.

At that time, Yeltsin's name didn't ring a bell in my ears, nor were his alternating scowls and smiles familiar to my eyes. He had been in Moscow scarcely a year, having been brought in from his party secretary's post in Sverdlosk by Gorbachev to clean up the Moscow party organization. Having earned a reputation for attention to detail, meeting the citizenry, hard work and other unconventional leadership attributes, Yeltsin was nicknamed "the City Hall Tsar". He quickly made a name for himself, which in Soviet politics means he quickly created a number of internal enemies. His bold policies and tenacious style collided with the inertia of the all-powerful city bureaucracy. His dismissal of senior apparatchiks and his candid expressions to the

Western media brought him under scrutiny by the Politburo, of which he was a candidate (non-voting) member. "Of course. they discussed me when I wasn't there," he writes.

Within the year Yeltsin was creating waves for Gorbachev too. After roundly criticizing his mentor for the slow pace of reform of the economy and the party, Gorbachev struck back, attacking Yeltsin as reckless and pompous. In the old-fashioned way, Yeltsin was forced to retract his most scathing remarks, and more importantly, to resign his post as first secretary of the Moscow party organization, the city's top executive position. He was unceremoniously kicked off the Politburo three months later, but was thankfully offered the post of first deputy chairman of the State Construction Committee. He notes in pre-Glasnost days this would have been unthinkable. In fact, all through the book Yeltsin generously credits Gorbachev for the fundamental changes in Soviet thinking. It is for not going further that Yeltsin has now, not ironically, been elevated as the main opposition force to the beleaguered Soviet leader.

This account of his life, however, should be judged with suspicion. It was hastily written and produced, no doubt at the behest of Simon & Schuster's publicity department. Yeltsin candidly admits that up until the convening of the second Congress of People's Deputies in late 1989, "the time for summing up," hadn't yet arrived. The book suffers as a result. Not only is it too short, it also lacks an index and any annotations. Moreover, the editing is sloppy, the book apparently not having been assigned to a professional translator due to its innumerous examples of awkward wording and incorrect syntax. Yet apart from these problems, (never mind the two factual errors on the book's jacket copy) Yeltsin tells some interesting stories.

After brief forays into episodes from his youth, and about his family, and their collective farming community in the Urals, Yeltsin wisely concentrates the bulk of his writing on the events following Gorbachev's advocacy of Perestroika in the Spring of 1986. He dwells at length on the first elections to the reformed Soviet parliament in March and April 1989, and offers the first ever insider's view of the campaign trail. He does an admirable job of explaining the heretofore secret methods of top-echelon decision making, freely praising and damning both policies and personalities along the way. His disdain for Gorbachev's inaction is attributed to his revulsion for the strength-sapping, vision-skewing qualities of power. "Gorbachev liked to hear himself talk," concludes Yeltsin, "though he frequently had nothing to say." The failings of the Soviet leadership are not from a lack of ideas, he maintains, but from a reluctance to stand behind them and take responsibility for the consequences.

The author could be faulted for glossing over such important issues as his heart ailment, the war in Afghanistan, the Chernobyl nuclear disaster and the causes of ethic dissension across the expanse of Soviet frontiers. He makes up for these deficiencies by describing his rise to power, his struggle against bureaucratic malaise and his remarkable comeback from the political equivalent of Siberia. In one passage. he writes:

"To make a career in the party... a person must excel at adapting his personality and convictions to whatever is required by the powers that be at any given moment. He must be dogmatic and learn to do or say one thing while thinking something else."

It is exactly this sense of hypocrisy, characterized by Gorbachev himself, that doomed Yeltsin into becoming the bully-boy of Soviet politics. "It is my belief," he writes, "that if Gorbachev didn't have a Yeltsin he would have to invent one." By keeping him near the center of power but away from the party and federal machinery, Gorbachev plays the "wise omniscient hero" to Yeltsin "the madcap radical". Judging from recent developments, it's a role he relishes. By championing the interests of the people over those of the state, Yeltsin immodestly predicts the complete collapse of the Soviet governmental system without his manner of reforms. His predictions increasingly appear to be correct.

Since this book was released in 1990, Yeltsin has officially quit the Communist Party, been elected President of the Russian Republic and became the only serious opponent to Gorbachev's (and the Communists' continued rule. In recent weeks, he has challenged his president to resign, forged an independent inter-republic foreign policy and gained the power to rule by decree within Russia. With mounting strikes, food price hikes in the wake of food shortages and ever-simmering nationalist and ethnic unrest, Gorbachev's likely successor must be watched and understood intently. Yeltsin's musings and views make absorbing reading, even if they were crafted to broaden his international appeal.

REQUEIM FOR A LIGHTWEIGHT

Gorbachev Knocks Himself Out of the Ring

As the National Chairman of the Mikhail Gorbachev Fan Club of North America I feel particularly qualified to assess his career, even if it turns out that it's a short one - - a prospect I very much anticipate (and lament). With the Soviet Union evaporating before our very eyes, and with the rise of nationalist leaders like Boris Yeltsin in Russia and others in the republics, it's rather obvious that Gorby's (that's what we call him) days are numbered. Tough luck for the man who turned the world back from the brink of nuclear annihilation.

Gorbachev rose through the ranks of the Communist Party like all other members of the Central Committee. He is obviously a smart and tough politician to have climbed to the top of that august body at the comparatively tender age of 53. He was, as many of his colleagues were, a devoted Communist who ardently believed the Party had digressed from its progressive role in society. As a result, he's been called a reformer; as a consequence of his reforms, he's been labeled a destroyer.

Of course, he was neither. After it's all said and done, I believe Mikhail Gorbachev will be remembered as a man who happened to be at the right (or wrong, depending on your view) time and place to affect an influence in the process of cataclysmic change. He did the best he could, but under such circumstances as the collapse of an empire, no one would likely have done any better. To be sure, we are very fortunate that a man with Gorbachev's temperament was at the helm as the change occurred. It might have been more bloody if he weren't.

In the cold hard world of objective facts and empirical statistics, Gorby was the world's biggest political loser. Under his five-year stewardship the U.S.S.R. went from an international superpower to an international beggar. Her foreign alliances evaporated. Production and exports dropped by margins exceeding fifty percent. Political upheaval and social ferment, once entirely absent, skyrocketed to extremes. The once ironclad union started breaking apart like a crumbling cake in his clumsy clutches. It's a scenario we all know and marveled at. But Gorbachev hung on.

Openly criticized at home, his fortunes dwindling abroad, Gorby kept Lenin's dream alive by lecturing his friends and appeasing his foes. He held his head high even as many threatened to chop it off. In order to keep a measure of peace and sanity, he waffled between true reform and maintaining the status quo. Yet such moves were a gamble and it appears that he has lost all he wagered.

To most of his countrymen Gorby was a blunderer. Having failed to embrace significant economic reforms, he alienated the increasingly deprived working classes. But flirting with Western notions of free enterprise he angered his erstwhile Communist comrades. Facing attacks from both liberals and conservatives, he waged a lonely battle playing one side off against the other. It was a balancing act he failed to master. In the end, he created no greater sin than under estimating his adversaries and over estimating his allies. Many a great man in history made similar mistakes.

To many in the West, having first shaken off their early infatuation, Gorby was a victim overwhelmed by inexorable forces which he unleashed but could not control. With each successive crisis, he became increasingly paralyzed. Not knowing where to turn, he stumbled along with one foot in the past and the other in the future. In so doing, he squandered what he had left of our affection. In contrast our sympathy for him and his nation rose. But like a fire consuming a house, the damage was too extensive to consider trying to save him. Gorbachev had become politically irrelevant.

What's left then of Gorby, and the policies of Glasnost and Perestroika he championed?

Glasnost unleashed the drive for democracy and freedom which even now pulls apart the nation. Perestroika plunged the economy into the abyss to the extent that it seems pointless to try and resuscitate it. Is Gorby to blame for this state of affairs? Of course, he is! Had he not championed the idea of reform, even if his ideas were far different than those that ultimately prevailed, the Red Empire might just as well have survived. In that instance, the world would still be an atomic powder keg and the Cold War would likely be raging. Thus, Gorby, for all of his faults, for all of his mistakes, rendered us all an invaluable service. He freed his nation from seventy odd years of totalitarian rule. He freed humanity from the feat of a nuclear holocaust.

What more can a guy do?

Gorby, we love you. Promise us you'll enjoy your retirement.

HIS CAREER AT A GLANCE

These are among Mikhail Gorbachev's accomplishments and failures during nearly seven years of leading the Soviet Union:

Accomplishments

- Opened the door to political liberalization.
- Strengthened the elected legislature.
- Released political prisoners.
- Lifted news media restrictions.
- Allowed freedom of travel.
- Let East European allies break away from the Soviet system.
- Pulled troops out of Afghanistan and ended other proxy wars.
- Negotiated drastic cuts in nuclear and conventional armed forces by superpowers.

Failures

- Moved too slowly on economic reforms.
- Partial steps worsened shortages of food, fuel, housing and consumer goods.
- Didn't give republics enough autonomy.
- Underestimated Boris Yeltsin's appeal and mishandled attempts to remove him.
- Chose aides who turned against him, including his vice-president, KGB chief, defense minister and prime minister.
- Lost key allies such as Foreign Minister Eduard Shevardnadze, and economist Stanislav Shatalin, who became frustrated with hesitation on reform.

Part III
PLACES

A view of Arbat Street in central Moscow. The name of the surrounding neighborhood is known as The Arbat.
Photo courtesy of Novosti Press Agency

ARBAT: THE SOVIET SOHO

The Heart of Moscow is Full of Soul

> Look, pedestrians, this poem
>   was written for you.
> The authorities gave us a lavish
>   present, an undeclared decree
> To give dissenters
>   and free thinkers
> An "honorable" place in the bestiary where
> Muscovites and Provincial fools and
>   foreigners are hanging out!
>
> Tatayana Kostanzhogolo,
Street Poet

The Arbat is a street and district in central Moscow. A long lane which begins at a spacious square and ends at the Stalinist-gothic building of the Ministry for Foreign Affairs, the Arbat is flanked by narrow side streets in 18th century European style. it is regarded as the SoHo of the city, the vanguard of everything new, cheeky and risqué in this newly liberated land.

Lined with booksellers, cafes, curiosity shops and aspiring artist stands, the Arbat is more like Paris or Amsterdam than Moscow. Street poets and musicians offer tip-if-you-will performances. Young people flock here to see each other, old folks hither forth for a serenade. Tourists can freely mingle with schoolgirls and gypsies here too. On a cool summer evening, it is the only place in this metropolis where any action is.

The Arbat became a pedestrian mall in 1985. It is one of the few popular decisions of the Moscow City Soviet (the city council). Its pre-revolutionary architecture has been largely restored, and modern lighting illuminates it deep into the night when the rest of the city is empty and still. Music, political discourse, the barks of vendors, the loud din of unhurried conversation echo through the cool summer air. The sharp eyes of caricature artists hunt for customers. Painters and craftsmen with items for sale watch hopefully as the multitude cross past their wares. Lovers embrace, bicker. Children scurry about. Beggars stand motionless with their cups out. It is a striking exhibition of the diversity that is the Soviet Union.

Along the cobblestones of the Arbat are several places worth visiting. The Prague restaurant, one of Moscow's finest, is at the west end of the Arbat, near its unofficial beginning. It's stylish red neon sign and grapevine stucco molding make it look as beautiful and its traditional Russian cuisine is tasty. However, trying to get reservations here is about as difficult as scaling the Kremlin Wall. Alexander Pushkin's five room apartment is now a museum and can be visited well into the evening. For theatre goers there is the Vakhantov Theatre, which stages production from the early autumn to early summer. A renovated orthodox church and Georgian cultural center are also on hand for casual visits. Dozens of memorial plagues are affixed to buildings where this or that Russian or Soviet hero lived or worked.

Sipping along the Arbat is fun but expect to pay top rouble for your purchases. Art and souvenirs are plentiful and generally overpriced. Be prepared to wait in line for anything good, however, as Muscovites have a peculiar knack for discovering where rare goods are being sold. Foreign currency shops, called Berozika (birch tree) stores are available for a wider selection of Russian-made and imported gifts.

Taverns are easier to come by here, but like bars everywhere in the Soviet Union, they have no variety of beverages and frequently even lack vodka and white wine. The same is true for food stores. Staples like bread, canned fish, fatty sausage and sugar cookies are relatively easy to come by, fresh fruit, poultry and fish are less commonly found. Remarked one local shopper, there's plenty of food for thought in the Arbat but almost no food for people.

THE ART OF SMUGGLING

New Museum Features Confiscated Art and Valuables

Brest, Byelorussia: In a small and stylish building on Lenin Avenue, in this Byelorussian city on the Soviet-Polish frontier, there recently opened a museum unlike any other. It's nicknamed the Smugglers Museum.

What makes it unique is that is comprises solely of art objects which were confiscated by Soviet customs authorities. Called simply, the Museum of Rescued Art Treasures, the museum houses an impressive exhibition ranging from jeweled flatware to priceless religious icons.

According to curator Katia Sarychihina, the idea for the museum came from a local journalist who visited the warehouse of the border police while researching a story on the illicit trade of used Soviet-made televisions to black marketeers in Poland. "Not only did he find a wall of televisions and radios," she said, "but he also chanced upon a box containing porcelain figurines. Next to it, wrapped in yellowed newspaper, he discovered six delicate angel-shaped candlesticks made of gold and crystal. In a corner of the building he noticed a barrel full of rolled up canvases."

"He made some inquiries and soon discovered there were hundreds of artistic items stored there without anybody realizing their value," she said. "To the police they were just articles of contraband. They were recorded in their ledgers and tucked away out of sight."

"Soon the newspaper wrote an editorial demanding that all such objects of art be fully disclosed and turned over to the public for the establishment of a museum. It took several years, but as you can see, we were successful in this endeavor."

The completed museum opened last March (sic. 1988). Not only does it exhibit the seized objects of art, it also reveals the clever methods which were employed to conceal them from detection. For example, a diamond studded 17th century clock is displayed next to the clay pot with a false bottom in which it was secreted. Elsewhere, two small painted icons are exhibited above a can of powdered milk inside which they were hidden.

Journalist Alexander Suvorov was one of those who promoted the idea of establishing the museum. "We were always a bit self-conscious of the fact that we could not afford a first-class museum collection like those in Minsk, Moscow and Leningrad," he said. "So when we learned about the many objects in the warehouse we immediately realized this was the answer to our problems."

Brest is an industrial city with a population of about 300,000. In pre-revolutionary times it was known as Brest-Litovsk and was the site of the 1918 treaty with Germany which took the infant Soviet state out of World War I. It has the dubious distinction of being the only Soviet city ever visited by Adolf Hitler.

Suvorov described the difficulties they were encountered in convincing the customs office to release the newly discovered items. It took the combined efforts of the city government, the Byelorussian Communist Party chief and a glasnost-inspired letter writing campaign initiated by the newspaper before the director of the department acquiesced.

"Fortunately," said Suvorov, "we don't have a law governing the disposition of confiscated antiquities. In such instances it is well established that all rights to the items revert to the public."

Slowly and over a period of several months, individual objects of art were released to a local commission which was formed to oversee the establishment of the museum. The commission was successful in obtaining a gingerbread-style building in the heart of the city. Soon afterward a green army truck delivered a load of assorted objects which exceeded even the most conservative expectations. Among the 450 items turned over to the commission were household furnishings from several tsarist palaces, oil paintings by Russian masters which were presumed lost in the war, and countless rare icons covering six centuries of Russian Orthodoxy. "The consignment was so large and varied that it was clear we underestimated the size of the building we would need," said curator Sarychihina.

Without patronizing its patron, the museum also depicts the exploits of the customs office and its techniques of uncovering smuggled artifacts. As such it serves as a warning to would-be smugglers that no matter how clever, they will be found out. It is a felony to remove art or icons from the Soviet Union without permission and declaration.

Museum of Rescued Art Treasures This old mansion, dating from the 1930's houses a huge collection of objects of art that have been confiscated from smugglers at the border crossing of Poland. It was opened in 1989.
Photo courtesy Brest Gazetta

MOLDAVIA DAZE

The Sleepy Soviet Republic Awakens

KISHINEV, Moldavia: Journalist Vychislav (Slava) Lagutin looks like a tourist from Scotland. His light complexion, carrot-colored hair and English accent give him away. But Slava of Moldavia is not either a Scit or a native Moldavian. He's a Russian who was sent to work here after completing his studies in journalism at the Foreign Language Institute of Moscow State University. Like all Russians here, he is a prisoner of his nationality, the hated personification of 45 years of penned up anti-Soviet sentiment. But he's a likeable rascal so he encounters fewer problems than most.

Slava and I have a few days off from our touring. Together we have visited the span of the European portion of the U.S.S.R. We started in Leningrad and two months later ended in Volgograd. We've covered 12,000 kilometers by train. (I always got the top bunk.) We've become close friends, and I'm amazed that he knows the lyrics to Beatles' songs better than I do. He promised to show me around Kishinev, the capital city on the River Bic in this formerly peaceful republic.

Moldavia is a poor and mountainous land of 4.4 million people. It was incorporated into the U.S.S.R. in 1940 as a consequence of the secret protocols to the 1939 Soviet-Nazi Non-Aggression pact. Prior to then it was a province in the kingdom of Romania called Bessarabia. Most of her citizens consider themselves closer to Romanians than

Russians; the native language is Latin-based, not Slavic. Moldavians seem determined to abandon the Soviet Union and make it on their own. Like the Balts, they feel they have a legal justification to declare their independence now that the parliament has declared the pact invalid. Her capital city was rebuilt following the war, and despite the unrest (perhaps on account of it), it was one of the more pleasant places I visited..

We ate at the finest restaurants because Slava has good connections. One was designed like a grotto, complete with medieval motifs and plates. We enjoyed a steam bath, an ice bath and a massage. We watched as a demonstration, something new here, marched up Lenin Pospekt past the Central Committee building and heaved insults at militiamen standing guard. We visited the Museum of the Friendship of Peoples and learned more than one could ever want to know about the hundreds of nationalities which comprise of the Soviet population. We passed an afternoon playing chess in Slava's office. We're about even but his driver Ivan massacred us both.

Our first excursion was to the city of Tiraspol high in the hills of the Eastern Carpathian Range. It's a sleepy city of 100,000 people, not remarkable except for her local vineyards and muddy streets. Fifty kilometers out of town we stopped by a lovely but not-so well-known beach along the banks of the River Dniester. We swam and laughed, and threw stones at the old tugboats we occasionally saw pass. We also drank a lot of red wine. Before long Ivan was snoozing and neither Slava nor I could see straight. Accordingly, we spent the night shivering in the backseat of the car. We awoke like Moldavia herself, tired but anxious to get moving.

The following day we visited a monastery and paid tribute to monks who perished trying to save it from the flames of a Nazi incendiary bomb. The roof collapsed on top of them while they were rushing to save the art and icons. Sadly, they were not able to save the manuscripts, books and paintings that were stored for centuries in its library. It was a grim reminder how art and culture are lost to the flames of war. The head monk told me his Franciscan order had a chapel and friary in Vermont.

At this new restaurant, we enjoyed a lovely meal of lamb shanks, saffron-scented rice and sugared parsnips. It is a transformed beer cellar beneath Kishinev's finest hotel, The Grand Plaza. Privately-owned establishments like this are beginning to open all over the country. Absent is any hint of Soviet rule or Communist Party propaganda. Naturally it was very crowded and the queue to be seated was hours long. However, we were seated at the owner's table in the kitchen when the prospect of an American guest paying with hard currency was made known. Hard currency (i.e. US dollars, German marks, British sterling, French francs, etc.) is highly prized and can be used to purchase items not otherwise available through official state-controlled distribution channels.
Photo by the author

He asked if I was able to deliver a box to it and I said I would be happy to if I received appropriate export permits and such. I suspected he wanted me to smuggle something out for him. I remembered the museum we had visited in Brest filled with art and antiquities that were confiscated by border guards. There is no way I wanted any part of the danger that prospect offered. I suggested it would be best for me to deliver a letter or some papers that I could easily pass off as my own. But he didn't take me up on my offer. Just as well, I thought. We were treated to a Spartan meal with five other monks and excused ourselves so they could retire to their prayers and farming.

In the late afternoon, as the sun began to wane in the western sky, a group of four friends of Ivan, all drivers I presumed, and Slava and I visited a spa in a picturesque village south of Tiraspol. It was my first experience in a traditional bathhouse where our bodies were manhandled beyond my comfort zone. We were washed, molded, squished, squeezed, lashed, scraped, and oiled. We were dunked in both boiling and frozen pools, alternately about a half-dozen times. And then we were served beer and sausages with fresh baked sweet rolls and some kind of tart jam with nuts in it. I would have preferred to stay at a guesthouse but that kind of request here needs advanced planning. So we made the long drive back to Kishinev while my new friends yammered on about things I likely couldn't imagine, but was endlessly curious about. The chubby one named Marco spoke a little English and said they were arguing about local sports teams. I naively presumed it had been about the excitement over local elections. Look to what a man treasures and there you'll find his heart.

Beyond these Gates the Earth Moans, so reads the entrance plaque at the stirring memorial to the Salaspils (salt fields) death camp near Riga, Latvia. Salaspils was one of the most ruthless and ghastly death camps of the war. Today all that remains is a plain punctuated with granite blocks marking the former workhouses and barracks. Above is an ensemble of three of the six solemn figures called, The Immortal Ones around which the complex is laid out.
Photo by the author

HONOR ETERNAL

War Memories Evoke Stirring Memories, Deep Emotions

Poklonnaya Hill spans along Kutuzovsky Prospekt in southwestern Moscow. It earned its historical significance in 1812 as the point on which Napoleon and his conquering army waited in vain for the Keys to the Kremlin, the symbolic token of Russian sovereignty. The ensuing Russian victory was commemorated by the dedication of a Triumphal Arch in Victory Square, which graces the broad boulevard named in honor of the heroic Russian general, Mikhail Kutuzov.

Upon the expanse of the hill itself a magnificent new memorial to the Second World War is now under construction. Entitled, "Monument to Victory in the Great Patriotic War 1941-1945," the memorial complex will comprise of a grandiose museum, a domed pantheon, a mourning hall, a 500 meter-long heroes colonnade, a monumental statue, and hundreds of sculptures, murals and fountains sprawling over 300 acres of surrounding parks and gardens. To avoid dwarfing the Square and Arch, the planners have ingeniously incorporated them into the overall design. The entire complex is scheduled to be unveiled on May 9, 1995 on the 50th anniversary of Victory Day.

Though many years have passed, the memory of the Great Patriotic War, as World War II is known here, still burns deeply into the hearts of the nation. Its staggering toll of death and destruction shaped an entire era—an era which is only now coming to a close. In the wake of national misery and grief, images of stone and bronze arose on battlefields and in death camps to glorify the fallen. In following years, thousands of memorials and monuments were dedicated across the vast Soviet heartland. Piskarvoskoye Necropolis and the Green Belt of Glory in Leningrad, Mamayev Kurgan in Volgograd and the Hero-Fortress in Brest are the most widely known. Other smaller sites capture the twin themes of tragedy and triumph in equally stirring expression. Collectively they form a moving portrait of the horrible events which culminated in the loss of over 20 million citizens. It is therefore no surprise that such memorials have become popular attractions for Soviets and tourists alike. The memorial complex on Poklonnaya Hill, being the only national memorial to the war, will, thus, become the crowning achievement in the commemoration effort.

Over these several pages you will see examples of but a few of the beautiful memorials that have been erected in remembrance of the sacrifices exacted from the nation and her people. They serve as an eternal reminder that war is more terrible and tragic than we survivors can imagine.

Rise Up!, the central sculpture in Darnista Woods Memorial Complex near Kiev, pays tribute to 68,000 victims of Nazi atrocities. Like many memorials it was designed by a contest winning art school and financed and constructed entirely by volunteers. It was dedicated in 1968.
Photo by Nikolai Chodin.

A detail from the National War Memorial on Poklonnaya Hill combining Victory Square, The Triumphal Arch and the Monument to Victory Memorial Complex. It will be formerly dedicated on the 50th anniversary of Victory Day, May 9, 1995. It is located on the western outskirts of Moscow near the front lines of both Napoleon and Hitler's invading armies. Photo courtesy of Anatoly Polanski, Chief Designer of the complex

The author at Mamayev Kurgan Memorial Complex in Volgograd. In the foreground is the surrial monument Fight to the Death, which was the battlecry during the defense of Stalingrad. Crowning the hill is the majestic Motherland statue rising over 60 stories high and features a museum at its base and an observation tower. During the epic battle control of the hill passed between the warring sides nine different times. It was so littered with blood and shrapnel that grass would not grow on it for ten years after the war's end. This vast complex contains forty memorial elements and was dedicated in 1967.
Photo by Yuri Ivanov

The Cemetery of Villages is situated in the Katyn Memorial Complex forty kilometers outside of Minsk. Each marker contains an urn of soil from each of the 187 Byelourussian farming villages which, like Khatyn, were torched and all their residents executed. On a rise overlooking the Cemetery is the artistic composition entitled, The Trees of Life. Within the boughs of the iron trees are the names of the 800 villages that refused to die. The complex was unveiled in 1967 and was awarded the State Prize for architectural design.
Photo by the author

The poignant Monument to the Kiev Dynamo Footballers commemorates one of the cruelest episodes in the great war. Upon learning that members of the famous Soviet soccer team were being held captive, the Nazis ordered a game be played against the Luftwaffe team. The resulting "death match" saw the underdog Ukrainian team win, 5-3. The enraged Germans imprisoned the victors and executed four team members who scored the goals. The monument was dedicated at the new Dynamo Stadium in 1971.
Photo by the author

The port of Odessa is one of the largest sea ports on the Black Sea. It was occupied by the Nazis for seven months in 1942 and features a navel memorial on its waterfront promenade. Today it is the Soviet Union's Western Gateway and a commercial lifeline for the importation of goods from Europe, both east and west.
Photo by the author from a naval helicopter

ODESSA: THE RED BLACK SEAPORT

Teaming with Shoddy Goods and Life's Contradictions

The southern Ukrainian city of Odessa is the largest Soviet port on the Black Sea. Just as Leningrad (as St. Petersburg) was dubbed the Russian Empire's "Window to the West," Odessa was dubbed its "Western Gateway" due to its historical commercial importance. And like Leningrad, Odessa was the beneficiary of more than two centuries international trade, visitation and developmental vision. Though hardly befitting its reputation as the capital of the Soviet Rivera, it's a beautiful city designed and maintained to typify 19th century Russian provincialism.

Yet it's awfully tattered too. Behind her impressive decorated facades are dilapidated buildings with over-crowded courtyards filled with hanging laundry and stray cats. Odessa's busy and colorful streets, once grand and imposing, are now mostly victims of neglect and urban decay. It's a problem all large Soviet cities have yet to come to grips with. Yet with that said, Odessa is a fine place to visit. There are numerous sights for tourists to enjoy, including the Archaeological Museum which houses the world's largest collection of Egyptian, Grecian, and Roman relics under one roof. Dating back to 1825, it is but one of the many palatial buildings that were built here to please so many long-forgotten Russian aristocrats. The Opera House nearby is another. It was designed by two Viennese architects and opened in 1887 with Tchaikovsky conducting.

The highlight of any visit to Odessa is the harbor, and the Potemkin Steps which descend to it from Pushkin Square. The square, named in honor of Russia's most famous (and celebrated) poet, who lived in exile here in 1823-24, is now a beacon for enterprising young Soviet businessmen. One can be photographed against the bay here, have their fortune told, or be carried up and down the steps here for just a couple of roubles. It is traversed by Primorsky Boulevard, a handsome pedestrian mall that serves as a crosswalk from which to view the panoramic harbor below. It was here in 1905 that the crew of the battleship Potemkin mutinied in support of a worker's strike, only to be gunned down by troops loyal to the Tsar. the action was brilliantly recreated in Sergei Eisenstein's famous 1925 silent film named in honor of the ship. The gruesome impressionistic dramatization of the massacre upon the steps subsequently lent them the ship's name too.

The people of the city of Odessa suffered greatly during the Great Patriotic War, which is how the Soviets refer to a World War II. With the Germans in control of the sea, the city was blockaded for two years and shelled mercilessly. Odessa was also the headquarters of the Russian navy during the Crimean War (1853-1857) which pitted Tsar Nicolas I against the combined navies of Turkey, Britain and France, ending inconclusively when all sides suffered more damage than the fighting was worth. It did, however, check Russia's quest to absorb territories from the weakening Ottoman Empire. During the post-Revolution civil war too, Odessa was occupied by pro and anti-Soviet forces anxious to control her port and rail facilities.

While yesterday's Odessa is interesting to experience, today's city is more intriguing by far. The much-heralded "era of renewal" has woke up what must have been three or four decades of bureaucratic slumber. The city is leading all others in the Ukraine in new business start-ups, population growth and job creation. Tourism accounts for over half of the new activity, but light industry, food processing and mineral excavation also rank high on the cities' plans for the future. It's about time, many cry. What good is a seaport which cannot deliver a single lobster, crab or shrimp dinner to money-spending travelers?

Odessa's newest attraction is a sprawling flea market which takes place every weekend on 175 acres about ten miles north of the city center. To this barren, fenced-in facility flock hundreds of thousands of bargain hunters, each anxious to find this or that object of capitalist creation no Soviet enterprise has been industrious enough to manufacture. Vendors line long and narrow alleys displaying items purchased mostly by merchant mariners on their trips abroad. Their wares are without exception simple and ordinary, yet they command exorbitant prices. A pair of corduroy slacks (which look used) costs the equivalent of two weeks' wages. Shoes and boots cost even more; small appliances such as a blender, a toaster and a countertop oven are ridiculously overpriced, but they sell too. Boom boxes and VCR cassettes are clearly the most sought after products.

So gerry-rigged is the market that hardly any vendors have stalls from which to conduct their operations. Most simply place their goods on old newspapers which they spread on the ground. They are eagle-eyed, and security is heavy due to the frequent theft and arguing over goods and prices. Standing at one end of the market one sees a virtual ocean of humanity floating through the selling lane, looking over the picked-over remainders. One needs to arrive before dawn to be assured any reasonable selection of goods. Even then the crowds that gather make the entire sojourn one gigantic commotion of hope and frustration. It is a crucible of the entire Soviet Union.

Elsewhere around Odessa is a rural sweep dotted with collective farms, paper and steel mills and small factories that churn out tractors, radios and windows. A large chemical plant near the Green Belt of Glory, a system of war monuments that hallmark significant land battles, is a named after American industrialist and Sovietophile Armand Hammer, whose Occidental Petroleum corporation helped set it up.

Other inland areas house characteristically Soviet-style apartment blocks, and supporting facilities like stores, clinics and schools. But it is the coastal plains for which Odessa is most popular. Several popular beaches can be accessed either by auto, rail or ferry. There are also many parks, each with its own restaurants and playgrounds. The main port offers passenger ship service to numerous international cities, but more commonly to the Crimean Peninsula and resorts of Yalta, Sochi and Batumi.

THEY CAME TO STAY

A Handful of Americans Adopt U.S.S.R. as New Home

About the last person you'd expect to bump into in Orel, Russia is someone from your hometown. Yet that's exactly what I did while visiting this moderately-sized metropolis 300 kilometers south of Moscow.

Her name is Cheryl Brown and she teaches English language classes as a local tourism industry training college. She's lived in Orel for six years, and in the Soviet Union for a total of eleven. What brought her from Detroit to Orel? "Love, what do you expect," she ruefully admits. "But it didn't work so I got a job and have stayed here ever since. I visit my family every couple of years, and last year my brother and sister-in-law came to see me. They were astonished to see how well I'm getting along here."

Larry Aldrich is another transplanted American residing on Soviet soil. He coaches a men's and women's basketball team in Kiev, the capital of the Ukraine. Larry has been here only 18 months but he expects to stay as long as he's needed. "It's hard to describe my life in a way that would sound interesting," said Larry. "There are a lot of things I do not like here and, of course, I miss the things back home (Fort Worth, Texas) but I'm happy."

A general, indescribable happiness is the reason most Americans who live in the U.S.S.R. offer when confronted by this intrepid (and disbelieving) reporter's questions. That's the same conclusion reached by another transplanted Yank, Paula Garb, an anthropological historian who wrote a book about them several years ago. Writes Garb: "Americans who choose to reside in the Soviet Union almost always do so out of preference as opposed to circumstance. They are largely content and well adjusted, and rarely admit to missing the apple pie and motherhood themes represented by the United States of America."

While the Soviet authorities refuse to cite numbers, the U.S. Embassy in Moscow estimates that 15,000 Americans live across the expanse of the U.S.S.R. Most moved there due to marriage, others for jobs and research and scientific opportunities. In the 1960's admits Garb, "Moscow's chief subway engineer was from Minneapolis! "The country's poor economic climate is the greatest disincentive for remaining," she said. "With expanding foreign investment and trade agreements there will be more and more American's living here," said Garb. "Hopefully conditions will improve so that some will feel welcome to stay."

Paul Jacobs is one such new arrival. His company operates a new chain of Western-style quick-print shops in Moscow and Leningrad. He finds life in the Soviet capital both fun and depressing. "There's lots to do here, especially if you have foreign currency like me. Women especially want to get to know me. How can a guy argue with that?" he said smiling.

Still, in sheer numbers the Americans living in the U.S.S.R. are a far cry from the tens of thousands who traveled here during the 1920's and 30's. At that time Ford Motor Company and others were hired to build automobile factories and other plants in the newly founded Communist state. Their employees and families were settled in large communities with their own facilities and schools.

While most left before the war, some stayed and blended into Soviet society. Stalin's insistence that they take Soviet citizenship scared others away. "I would never have guessed I'd be living here," said Linda Houser Shelepin, a mother and nurse in the city of Volgograd. She met her husband Igor, a fireman, while studying at Volgograd

University in the early 1970's. She could have emigrated with him to the U.S. but decided to stay in deference to his family, which was dependent for support on his wages and preferential housing rights. "No matter what you hear, life is simpler here," she said. "I went home (Burlington, Vt.) for a month-long visit and I actually got homesick. That's when I realized I had made the right decision."

Are they suspected of working for the CIA? "Yes," answers Alexander Moore, whose father moved to the Soviet Union in 1957, during a thaw in the Cold War. "We used to be followed, and my dad had to report weekly to the local militia office. There was a general paranoia about Americans back then, that they wanted to encircle and then destroy the U.S.S.R. Lee Harvey Oswald wanted to stay but he didn't fit it in so he went back to the USA and look what happened. Imagine if he had stayed." After thinking a little more, he continued, "That feeling has thankfully passed, now everyone just wants to be friends."

Says Larry Aldrich: "These people are not friendly in the American fashion. They won't go out of their way to help a stranger. But once they get to know you, you are enfolded into their world and become family to them. I find that comforting because I never had a real family back home. Now I have got dozens of them."
Photo by the author

Part IV
POLITICS

The YEAR 1989

Reverse Domino Theory in Action

"No government can long survive if it is based on lies."
Eduard Shevarnadze, Soviet Foreign Minister, April 4, 1988

Perhaps the strangest fact about the collapse of Communism in 1989 is that, even though it was frequently predicted, nobody believed it would really happen. If the Soviets had done anything well it was to create an image of itself as a modern, self-sufficient, monolithic superpower. What cracks might have existed in the Iron Curtain were thought to be patched up by the application of equal parts of force and bluster. The Party knew how to deal with dissent and it did so.

Yet, beneath the veneer of power there was turbulence in the Soviet ship of state, and in those of her Eastern bloc neighbors. Communism, standing in shame of its lofty aims, proved as politically bankrupt as it was economically inept. It was simply incapable of competing in the universe of ideas that modern technology transmitted to the ends of the earth. The entire system lay in tatters, ready to fall apart completely. National morale plummeted. A mood of anger and disgust descended across Eastern Europe. Despite Marx's best intentions, Communism proved unworkable, unlikeable and directly contrary to the very thing it most ardently sought to change: Human Nature.

A lesson could have been learned from the fall of the Roman Empire. Brute strength is only as powerful as the ruler who yields it is wise. Communist rulers from Lenin on down were most unwise and accordingly their hold on power weakened. If history has taught us anything, it is that a people can only be enslaved so long before they rise up and dispose of the source of their misfortune. That's what happened throughout Eastern Europe in 1989. The people found a voice and it said, "We've had enough!" Thankfully they were "assisted" by a Communist reformer, who, though he might not have known where he was going, knew exactly what he was fleeing from.

Gorbachev and the enormous task that lay before him cannot really be understood unless one realizes what life under Communism was like. Most of us are aware of the commonly expressed frustrations about lack of food and housing, but few are aware of the daily assault on reason perpetrated against the people by their corrupt and incompetent leaders. As one commentator suggested, life under Communism can only be measured by degrees of unbearability. Those captured in its grip grew tired of eating only "Brezhnev soup". Their lives were molded by forces over which they had virtually no control, and therefore no love was lost when those forces were ultimately defeated.

Communists see—or should we say, saw—the world through philosophically "tainted" glasses. They proceed from a belief that history is driven by the confrontation of class struggle—a struggle which the working classes are bound to keep losing unless united under the banner of International Socialism. Since it was the world's first socialist state, the U.S.S.R. and its Communist rules sought to be a catalyst for world revolution. Thus, from 1918 onward they embarked on a single-minded mission, backed by the skillful use of infiltration and propaganda, to instill a revolutionary zeal into the workers of the world. That ardor, charged as it is with pathos and promise, quickly ignited political and nationalistic passions around the globe. Only the U.S., backed by a bevy of allies best described as "strange bedfellows," created any obstacle to Communism's rapid, rabid spread.

Communism is more than a collection of economic and political doctrines. When combined with the precepts of Leninism and Stalinism, it became monotheist state religion governed by a single party dictatorship in which dissent is tantamount to heresy. The high priests of Communism fashioned deceptive liturgies in the names of deities named Karl Marx, Friedrich Engels and most importantly, Vladimir Ilyich Lenin. Many martyrs fell in the name of freedom; many more were dispatched to eternal glory. Yet, the overwhelming majority remained faithful to Communist dogma. Tolerance not being one of its chief virtues, it's no surprise. Conformity, as in any religion, was a measure of one's faith.

Were the people of Eastern Europe guilty of cowardice in remaining silent for so long? Hardly. Communism's grip over their minds and movements was keenly systematic and indiscriminately complete. While virtually shut off from the rest of the world by the fabled Iron Curtain, they stewed in a pot which cooked them into helpless victims of cruel, unfeeling state bureaucracy. Is it any wonder it took 45 years for the pot to boil over?

Theirs was a world where $2 + 2 = 5$ if the Party said it did. Friends spied on friends to curry favor with the bosses, the ever present "they" in Russian and other languages. Families were dispossessed "in the interests of the proletariat" and workers practiced "self-criticism" to avoid disgrace. Entire peoples were oppressed and imprisoned in the name of "overcoming distortions in social relationships". Artists and writers were continually admonished to steer clear of "bourgeois filth, Western decadence and perverted capitalist-imperialist notions of truth and justice". Under Communism schoolchildren faced mandatory reading assignments from tomes like Lenin's Issues in Dialectical Materialism. Meanwhile, in factories and farms their parents were forced to participate in political education seminars, which typically consisted of three hours' worth of lectures "followed by fervent and impassioned discussions in which unanimous resolutions were adopted". It's a world where food shortages are blamed on "distribution requirements," and where crime is labeled an unnatural social phenomenon caused by excessive class consciousness". It's a society where "connections" are worth more than currency, where exploding television sets account for 50% of all fires and in which the Berlin Wall is accepted as, "The Anti-Fascist Protective Barrier".

But the absurdity of "Wordspeak"—as George Orwell coined the nonsensical use of language and logic in his allegorical novel about Communism, *1984*—is by no means the only oddity in a Communist society. Logic and rationale are daily turned upside down to fit the edicts of the all-knowing, all-powerful Party apparatus. For example, nations proclaiming to be worker's paradises strangely prohibit independent labor unions, collective bargaining or the right to strike. These are unnecessary, the Communists claim, because the workers are in charge there. Medical care, while nominally free, was an illusory benefit. Out-dated methods and facilities, as well as a shortage of medicines, trained staff and hospital beds, left the people bereft in time of sickness. What good is free surgery if one has no confidence in the doctor? Similarly, the government subsidies for food and consumer staples was nonsensical to the consistent unavailability of product. Waiting in line became an unofficial pastime, the only commodity in ample supply being the number of benign things labeled "state secrets."

Over time, methods to circumvent the general, though largely silent dissatisfaction with life surfaced. Cynicism grew in proportion to anger. Alcoholism became pervasive. Official slogans were scoffed at. Many embraced strange beliefs in such things as psycho-spiritual healing and the glorification of poets and folk heroes. Young people, frustrated and unhopeful, dropped out of society, refusing to participate as a means of expressing their discontent.

Then there is the bizarre phenomenon of the Black Market, or as some refer to it, the "shadow economy." While officially illegal, it was apparently tolerated for preforming a larger social good—allowing for the letting off steam. In a country where goods and services are as scarce as ghosts, the following transaction actually took place: In order to get a nifty toy tank for her 7-year-old son, a mother took a job as a beautician in a salon. In exchange for tinting the hair of a local Party functionary, the mother obtained much sought-after theatre tickets. She traded the tickets to the manager of a shoe store for a pair of leather boots. She then bartered the boots to an auto parts huckster for a fender and a steering wheel. She lugged the two items to the toy store loading dock and offered them to the shipping clerk in exchange for the toy tank. She got it all right, but was perturbed to learn she could have achieved the same result with a cigarette lighter and a window crank. To over three hundred and fifty million captives of Communism, that's shopping!

In most countries of the world bribery is a crime; in Communist countries, it's an art. But unlike elsewhere, the worst thing to bribe an official with is cash. Communist currencies are useless because there is nothing to spend it on. The most effective means of exchange are Western brand products like Marlboro cigarettes, nylon stockings or video cassettes. Oddly enough, the most frequently bribed people are not Party officials, but apartment building superintendents, food shop managers and other purveyors. It's therefore no surprise to find auto mechanics, dairy farmers and vineyard keepers among the richest and most privileged people in Communist nations. Bribing policemen is also common. Usually simple items like chewing gum or disposable razors will suffice. The problem is that there are so many of them. Spend a leisurely afternoon in Moscow park and one will see officers dressed in uniforms of a dozen different designs. This is due to two reasons; First, the Communist penchant for creating symbols of authority. There's the militia, the traffic police, walking patrols, subway security guards, Ministry of Interior street squads and, of course, the KGB. Each separate authority has its own colors, insignia and decorations. The key is not to tell them apart, but to whom one should offer the highest bribe. The prevailing rule is the quality of their boots and the size of their belt buckles improves with importance. Anyone outfitted in less than genuine leather and polish gold-plat is not worth approaching. The second reason there are so many uniformed officials walking in the streets is actually two reasons in one. Since there is officially no or little crime, and since it is well known that nobody works in Communist countries, there's painfully little else for them to do. It's no wonder then that in the Soviet Union it is easier to get arrested than find an ice Cube—even in the winter.

Such is the world that Communists created. Experience shows, however, that Party leaders are not immune from the monster they helped create. They exist on a tight wire. Any member could be denounced and removed by an opponent or in a wholesale purge at the whim of the upper echelons. There are no momentary setbacks in the career of a Party official. One is either in the good graces of his superiors or he's liable to suffer a personal disaster like a one-way ticket to political oblivion, to Siberia or perhaps to both. Due to the Party's pyramidal hierarchy, one is always safest at the top. Party bosses are well known for hypocrisy and pomposity. Their fondness for privilege and prestige is easily explainable in a world where scarcity and apathy are the norms. They are typically lazy, uneducated, undignified and most dangerously, power-hungry. But they knew how to wield power, even if they did so incompetently.

The Soviet secret police, the KGB, the GRU, and their Eastern European counterparts have escaped criticisms of incompetence. On the contrary, they were regarded as the best and most efficient intelligence services in the world. More correctly, however, they are a tool, as a hammer is, used by the Party to beat down opposition and dissent. As a consequence, Eastern Europeans know well the meaning of a knock at the door at 3:00 a.m. A joke from Poland illustrates their ruthlessness: A worker is falsely convicted of "Anti-State Activities." Upon entering prison, his cellmates ask him how many years he was given. "Twelve years," the worker replied. "For what?" they ask. "For nothing, that's what," the angry worker said. The cellmates stood in disbelief. "You're lying," said one, "the most they give you for nothing is five years!"

Espionage is one of the KGB's specialties. It is particularly adept at obtaining Western military secrets by means of cunning, subterfuge or outright threat. Until recently it was not uncommon in the Soviet Union, East Germany and Romania to find the most attractive women on the secret police payroll. In exchange for designer clothes, cosmetics, and the like, they were typically employed to seduce foreign diplomats or visiting scientists and engineers to provide their paymasters with the power of blackmail. Soviet espionage resulted in the development of atomic and other weapons systems years before Soviet technology would otherwise been able, thus saving it tens of billions of roubles worth of research and development expense.

But the built-in contradictions of Communism were like a ticking bomb, ready to explode without notice. Gorbachev's reforms ignited the fuse. Despite the holding of remarkably free elections, social unrest swept the Soviet Union, threatening its very existence. Nationalist fervor and ethnic bigotry, long suppressed under one party rule, sprouted like weeds across the national landscape. Separatist movements gained popularity as official authority atrophied. The very notion of collective thinking, the foundation of their society, evaporated into thin air. "We changed overnight," said one Latvian reformer. "We had to, to avoid perishing." It was in this environment that the stunning events of 1989 unfolded. As the joke about the collapse of Communism goes: "It took ten years in Poland, ten months in Hungary, ten weeks in East Germany, ten days in Czechoslovakia and Bulgaria and just ten hours in Romania."

Whether change took place from the top down-as in the Soviet Union, Bulgaria and Hungary, or from bottom up-as in Poland, East Germany, Czechoslovakia and Romania, the result was the same: Communism was finished. The period of stagnation and distortion, as the pre-Gorbachev years are now officially described, was at an end. The willpower needed to hold the Soviet empire together had vanished. When asked why, Gorbachev advisor Alexander Yakolev replied, "We realized it was easier to change our policies than our people." Coming from a Politburo member, that's sobering testimony. It also helps explain exactly why 1989 unfolded as suddenly, and as surprisingly, as it did.

Nothing grabbed the world's attention like the opening of the Berlin Wall on the night of November 9. The fall of The Wall was East Germany's last-ditch effort to save itself from extinction. The previous three months had seen its society crippled by a mass exodus of its citizenry to West Germany. But like the proverbial floodgates of hell, once opened, The Wall could not be resealed. Before long East Germany was drawn like a magnet to its powerful Western brother.

A joke circulated that GDR. stood "Gradually Disappearing Republic," rather than German Democratic Republic.

Poland got a head start by ushering in democracy economic reform over a tumultuous, but gradual pace. Led by a freely elected Solidarity-controlled government, it embarked on a course of economic shock treatment to pave the way to a free market. Hungary and Bulgaria, taking the cue from Gorbachev's "new political thinking," introduced changes from within, harnessing their peoples' wrath before it could explode. Hungary's venture with so-called Gulosh Communism failed utterly and left it with the highest per capita debt in Eastern Europe. Bulgaria's orthodox approach caused it to be dubbed "the sixteenth Soviet republic." Under the gun of total breakdown, both nations struggled to identify "A Third Way."

In Czechoslovakia, student demonstrations and labor strikes forced the Party leadership to resign en masse. In just ten days a salvation government nominated a former political prisoner to be its new president. Free elections were immediately scheduled and the promise of rejoining the West enthralled her citizens to near frenzy. Romania bucked the trend of generally peaceable change in overthrowing the Ceausescu regime; it suffered a mini-civil war. Civil chaos followed the assumption to power of former leaders who claimed to have cleansed themselves of communist ideology. To assure their detractors they allowed a measure of plurality in a hastily convened "reform legislature." Yugoslavia, like the U.S.S.R., suffered a rapid process of fragmentation, or Balkanization, as it is known in those parts. With the tide of change occurring unevenly across its intra-national boundaries, long suppressed difference spewed forth. Only tiny Albania, the last vestige of Stalinism in Europe, escaped the decade without substantial change. But it would not escape it for long.

With Communism in collapse, the questions became: What would take its place? Will former Communists make good capitalists and good democrats? In the mad unraveling of their societies, as one system fell apart before a new one was put in place, is disorder sure to abound?

While the West has demonstrated a willingness to provide aid, nothing remotely like a new Marshall Plan will likely be forthcoming. The USA and the European community, paralyzed by worries of their own, were less reluctant in word than in deed. As a consequence, the former eastern bloc nations are largely on their own. How well or poorly they survive was the big question as 1990 began.

The YEAR 1990

Year One of the New World Disorder

"Getting rid of the Russians was the easy part."
—Arpad Goncz, President of Hungary,
July 13, 1990

If 1989 closed an era, 1990 surely opened another. As yet unnamed it was destined to be characterized by uncertainty. President George Bush began the year by proclaiming the birth of a New World Order. He heralded a post-Cold War partnership between the U.S. and the U.S.S.R. as the beginning of peace and prosperity for all. But with the latter being burdened by a crippled economy and internal unrest, it seemed unlikely the Soviets could pull their weight. For a moment it appeared clear, America was the world's only superpower, strong and invincible. Or was she?

Just as the Cold War bankrupted the Soviet Union, America was feeling the pinch too. With mile-high budget deficits, and domestic troubles too numerous to list, she could hardly be said to emerge from it unscathed. With her financial institutions wracked with losses, with her streets awash in violence and with her domestic tranquility threatened by budget deficits, spiraling debt, drug addiction, racial tension, mass incarceration and the spread of AIDS, America was in no condition for frivolity. In Washington, impassioned debate on how to spend the so-called Peace Dividend ended with the abrupt realization that such talk was folly. Even with significant cuts in defense spending, America was too far in the hole to help herself, let alone others in need.

Though the new decade began with promise, a flurry of international problems quickly sobered the most optimistic of souls. America had just launched its forces to oust a dictator from Panama, and faced the task of rebuilding a shattered nation. A world-wide economic downturn loomed. Civil wars in El Salvador, India, Israel, Cambodia, Liberia, Somalia and South Africa raged. Iraq invaded and annexed Kuwait, forcing an international coalition led by the U.S. to go to war to liberate it. And through it all, the Soviet Union continued its rapid, pitiful slide into anarchy.

To be sure, positive developments did occur. World War II officially came to an end in 1990. With the reunification of Germany, the dissolution of the Warsaw Pact, and the signing of a comprehensive set of new security agreements, the justification for the division of Europe ceased to exist. Symbols of the Cold War were put on the auction block. Weapons systems were destroyed under rigid verification regimes. Troop strengths were cut and both sides withdrew to decidedly more defensive positions. Parliamentary and other delegations were soon exchanging visits. The U.S. Information Agency and the National Endowment for Democracy sponsored crash courses in American-style governance for the curious from the East. Gorbachev even abandoned Castro's Cuba. Times had indeed changed. A feeling of relief pervaded the air. One set of challenges had been conquered; others seemed somewhat less menacing.

Behind the drawn Iron Curtain mayhem continued at a steady rate. The Soviet Union experienced a wrenching and seemingly endless national turmoil. While Germany gained unity, the Soviets were losing theirs. Fourteen of fifteen constituent republics declared independence or self-sovereignty. The symbols of Soviet authority and Russian hegemony were repudiated in successive waves of protest. Even Moscow's annual May Day spectacular was tarnished by demonstrators wielding banners such as "Down with the Red Fascist Empire," "72 Years on the Road to Hell," and "All Communists to the Dogs." Calamities erupted in Moldavia and the Baltic and Caucasus nations. The Central Asian republics underwent an Islamic and ethnic revivals. Perhaps most surprisingly, Russia and the Ukraine likewise expressed dissatisfaction with continued Soviet rule. As the national economy crumbled, so too did the power of central and regional authorities. The Red Army witnessed massive defections. Strikes and work stoppages regularly imperiled what little industry was still producing. Widespread dissatisfaction forced Gorbachev to continually reform his reforms, tossing him about like a buoy in a stormy sea. As he reduced the power of the Party over the economy, he strengthened his own by sounding the alarm of impending doom. "Everything is rotten now," said Gorbachev to the Supreme Soviet. "We are all rotten now." A more extraordinary and candid exclamation cannot be imagined.

Having to account for the condition of the country, Gorbachev admitted he had made great mistakes. Perhaps his greatest was the raising of expectations beyond his ability to deliver. This didn't inhibit him from frequently lashing out at his opponents in the Party and in the state bureaucracy. He excoriated "Enemies of Perestroika" and lambasted "the outrageous inefficiency of Soviet industry, agriculture and transport." Then, as a magician might pull a rabbit from a hat, he called for an end to the Party's "leading role" in Soviet society. The time for political plurality had arrived, democratic forces could no longer be held back. Some considered his pronouncement a watershed. In reality, it was but one more attempt to pacify his increasingly restless countrymen. But his magic hat proved empty. Gorbachev had embarked on a road but former dissident Andrei Sakharov predicted would lead to civil war and hardline military rule.

Elsewhere in Eastern Europe, ambitious new laws guaranteeing political, social and civil rights were implemented by a collection of novice coalition governments. Free elections were decreed. The right to practice religion was restored, as was the right to openly criticize the state. New political parties sprang up like mushrooms in a forest. They adopted unimaginative names like Civil Forum, New Forum, Democratic Forum, Democratic Union, Democracy Now, ad nauseum. One had to have the knowledge of a foreign journalist just to keep abreast of developments. Bulgaria had the Progressive

Liberals, and Hungary had the Liberal Progressives; Poland had both. Romania, for example, had 45 different certified political parties within sixty days of the toppling of the old regime. A noted political commentator suggested that a future U.S.S.R. could eventually give birth to as many as 5,000 separate parties, each with its own platform for reform.

Not only were these novice governments forced to contend with the breakdown of their societies, they also faced hyper-inflation, mass unemployment, food and fuel shortages, and a vast increase in lawlessness. Coalition after coalition braced to earn the public trust. Students and workers answered by organizing demonstrations and labor strikes. The heady days of cheer for defeating Communist dictatorships were lost in a moment, quickly overtaken by harsh realities and bitter truths. The standard of living spiraled ever-downward. And with each new step toward he creation of free markets, it seemed two steps backward were required as well. "It's like trying to make an aquarium out of fish soup," admitted Czech Foreign Minister Jeri Dienstbeir. The Eastern European nations, having long starved for democracy, quickly realized they had too much. Consensus and compromise, the high tenants of Western-style democracy, proved as elusive as the wind.

If there was agreement on anything, it was that there was no turning back. Communism as a way of life had been unalterably discredited. The future may not have looked bright but it was certain to escape the darkness of the past. From the rubble it wrought only shades of gray. Decades of mismanagement offered the opportunity for improvements, if only their economies could afford to finance them. The region saw the rise of the citizen-politician, the proliferation of new books and newspapers and a chance to "live the good life". Private enterprises sprang up to fill the vacuum for hard to find goods and services. Popular opinion assumed an appropriate role in the formulation of public policy. But as in the Soviet Union itself, the emerging democracies of Eastern Europe were suffocating from a cycle of political upheaval and economic chaos which fed on itself like a raging fire. In nations where democratic institutions were being formed without the benefit of democratic values, democratic solutions will be difficult to implement.

With little else to do but sit and watch, the U.S. and her European allies, augmented by the acquisition of East Germany, increasingly adopted a wait and see policy. Aid requirements were likened to a bottomless pit. Economic experts warned that Eastern European countries were liable to be turned into the equivalent of street corner junkies due to their dependence on foreign loans and credits. Serious doubts arose whether their ravaged systems could hold together, let alone generate growth. The West couldn't help but worry about what would become of the Soviet nuclear stockpile.

Before long, faith in new found freedom began to falter. Talk of the need for a "strong hand" ensued. The reform mayor of Leningrad chagrined, "The people do not believe in the possibility of solving their problems in a democratic way." A rising tide of intolerance deluged the U.S.S.R. Fearing an anti-semantic backlash, hundreds of thousands of Soviet Jews sought refuge in Israel. Ethnic clashes flared in Russia, Moldavia, Uzbekistan and Azerbaijan. In the Baltics, secessionist-minded governments refused to cooperate with Moscow, determined to leave the union completely. A fickle and faltering Gorbachev, having exhausted his bag of political tricks and being increasingly abandoned by his discontented legions, drifted rightward in an effort to pacify conservatives. The future of Perestroika seemed imperiled. As if to underscore the danger, Foreign Minister Eduard Shevarnadze, a staunch Gorbachev reformer, ended the year by abruptly resigning, warning that years of bickering and inaction made "the creeping of dictatorship" inevitable.

Has the Soviet Union come full circle? A military crackdown in Lithuania at the beginning of the new year offered an ominous picture of the future. Having spent three years in retreat, the Party apparatus seemed ready to lunge forward, if not to assert its preeminence, then to at least position itself as a force to be reckoned with. With its control over the army and security organs largely intact, it is a force to be reckoned with. Soviet expert Hendrick Smith may have described the situation most succinctly when he concluded, "De-Stalinization proved comparatively easy; de-Leninization will be infinitely more difficult."

UPWARDLY MOBILE COMMUNISTS STAND BY THEIR PARTY

Students at Higher Party School Accept Historic Change in Stride

Moscow: The morning after the Communist Party leadership announced its "leading role" (ie. "dictatorial role"), the sun rose pale and flat as ever over the gray of Moscow. And presumably, all the studious young Communists still showed up for their classes at the Higher Party School, eager as ever to catch up on the revised party dogma.

"I'm happy that I am living in this time," said Aleksander Lomachenko, a 34-year old party hopeful, putting aside his attaché case and armful of books and documents. He is anxious to earn the remaining degree credits he needs to earn the credentials to justify his job as deputy chief of one of the city's 33 district party committees. "It'll be so much easier to speak and mix with others after their doubts about the future of the party have been aired." He was pausing from his busy schedule in a long, high-ceilinged hallway adorned with portraits, photographs and busts of Communist heroes, a veritable iconography for passing students who seem completely unaffected by the party's reassessment of its future, and the promises the new policies may bring. It's a fitting environment for the students in training at this elite institute as they prepare themselves for Party achievement.

As the great human engine of this sprawling country, the Communist Party of the Soviet Union (CPSU) began another day of incumbency. But today is decidedly different. Today the 800-plus men and women who study here are quickly adjusting their conversations to reflect the Central Committee's historic announcement of its retreat from monopoly of power. More impressively, they exuded unflinching confidence that the Party, for all its turmoil, is still the place to be to launch their career paths. It's hard for them to believe any other institution can dislodge or replace the only seat of power they have ever known.

"There was a sigh of relief that it finally happened," said another student, Vladimir Boriskin, a 38-year old instructor from the Komsomol Central Committee. He is in his fifteenth year of Marxist studies. The Komsomol is the League of Young Communists, where the Party faithful who aspire to higher office must remain until age 40. "Of course, after this sigh comes a deep breath of air by which the people will be voicing demands for more progress on political and economic fronts," he said. "The impatience of our people is very high."

Indeed, Party mavericks like Russian Federation President Boris Yeltsin and other so-called "activists" said the Party's decision to renounce its claim on power is not enough to end Soviet political repression and control over the economy and social organizations. "It is necessary to eliminate party organs in the army, the police, the KGB, the courts, at schools, district soviets (local councils) and state institutions, "said Yuri Mityunov, a spokesperson for one would-be opposition party called the Democratic Union.

Not surprisingly, Yeltsin was the sole member of the CPSU's policy-making Central Committee to oppose the new political reforms, which were announced at an extraordinary national party conference called to convene by President Mikhail Gorbachev and held in early February, 1990. "I had grounds to vote against," the Associated Press quoted Yeltsin as saying. "But I think that the platform represents, if not a step, then a half-step forward and that reduces the tension in the country."

Inside the Higher Party School, where the corridors are immaculately polished and orderly, the students were generally mute with uncertainty, despite Boriskin's suggestion that debate is welcome. There was also some regret that the reform had taken so long to occur. "So many millions of lives could have been saved if this change would have come earlier," he said. When asked if he was referring specifically to the Stalin purges of the 1930's he said, "No. I mean since Day One until today." Then he added: "The crème of the nation was lost over and over again, with each generation."

But at the school's training center, unlike so many other places reeling with confusion for what the news portends, there is a feeling (perhaps a hope) that the Party's shift in course is not too late to prevent what they call here "a dinosaur's death." Everything may be calm on the outside but those in-the-know must realize that rapid change is in the air. The test will be how rapid and how chaotic. Says Lomachenko: "Since Stalin's time there was always been a negative feeling at opposition within *party ranks*. Hopefully this move will permit opposing voices to be expressed within new parties. It may take some time for this to emerge but it will happen."

"People just need to feel secure about expressing their opinions," he said. "And that's what true Glasnost is all about." After ten years of study he is learned enough to argue from biblical-like citations of Marxist-Leninist works that all is not lost. "It is a Leninist principle that approaches to politics must be flexible." Such rationalizations and intellectualizations will be common, no doubt. Lenin, like Shakespeare, can be quoted to stand of almost any proposition.

But it's doubtful that he and his other comrades at the school would have come to such an understanding a week ago.

Part V
ODDITIES

DEATH IN THE U.S.S.R.

Soviet Funerals and Cemeteries Set Their Own Standards

When someone we know dies we customarily visit the funeral home, the church and the grave site for the interment. We then follow with a wake held at a private hall or the home of the deceased. Dying is largely a private affair and the survivors are responsible for making all burial arrangements. Not so in the Soviet Union. In a nation characterized by central planning, death in the Soviet Union can be as hassle-ridden as life.

When a Soviet citizen dies, whether in a hospital or at home, or elsewhere, a first step is to notify the Office of Birth and Death Records in each municipality. This is the office which issues death certificates. The next step is to notify the local Bureau of Funerals and Cemeteries to arrange for burial. One may not register with the Bureau until a death certificate is in hand. With the customary slowness of any central governmental office, this is frequently a problem, especially for bereaving survivors in custody of the body.

Few funeral homes exist in the U.S.S.R. Those that do function with regularity are typically booked for years in advance for Party officials and union bosses and their families. The cost is also prohibitively high.

Most people pay their respects in the depart d's home where the body is laid out in pint-sized living rooms. Some civic buildings, cultural places and church parlors accept funeral parties, but they're few and far between. The overwhelming majority of Soviets make do with little or no complaints. Inc.

It's when one reaches the cemetery that the burial process becomes particularly burdensome. Cemetery plots are assigned according to where the person last lived; the family has no choice in this decision. (Determination is a more accurate description.) With restrictions on the number of dead that can be buried in any one day, and considering the long ground-freezing winters, getting the deceased buried can be a trying experience. If the family is lucky, the cemetery morgue will assume control over the body until an acceptable date can be found. Few families probably ever get to see their loved ones actually interred. This situation has caused a rampant black market in caskets.

The one aspect of dying in the U.S.S.R. which tops it in the U.S. is the Russian tombstone. Whereas pre-revolutionary cemeteries were plotted with iron fences dotted with the twin-crossed Orthodox Crucifix, modern cemeteries are spacious gardens with brilliantly created grave markers upon which is emblazoned an etched visage of the deceased. Others feature sculptured or original works of art. One can thus stroll through a Soviet cemetery as one would through portrait galleries. The addition of a face to the names and birth and death dates has a chilling, yet comforting effect on one. It may be the living's only solace in facing the death and burial process here.

VACATION TIME IS ALL TIMING

Peak Travel Season Lengthens Lines and Spurs Hustle for Tickets

Waiting in a line in the Soviet Union has become a frustrating fact of life. Whether one is attempting to buy food, find an apartment or purchase an automobile, the story has always been the same: Stand in line.

But of all the lines in the Soviet Union, the longest and the most frustrating ones are for train and plane passenger tickets during the peak summer and fall travel months. Railway stations and airline ticket offices all over the country are inundated by masses of holiday-seekers who will go to almost any length to secure the proper tickets. Authorities say the shortage of tickets breeds resentment, encourages graft and leads to mix-ups from the barter and exchange of tickets between erstwhile vacationers. In fact, demand has been so great that a thriving black market now exists exclusively for tickets and accommodations. Prices can often exceed 500 percent of the cost of the ticket.

It is well known that decades of economic mismanagement have caused wide-spread shortages and an inefficient service sector throughout the U.S.S.R. Indeed, the sorry state of the entire economy is seen as the leading reason for the current wave of unrest, which has manifested itself through ethnic violence and regional nationalism. It is the single biggest national issue at a time when a hailstorm of hitherto forbidden subjects is being openly and heatedly discussed. It's a problem that President Mikhail Gorbachev must solve if he is to succeed in his neo-revolutionary policy of Perestroika.

Under the leadership of Leonid Brezhnev, much of the public frustration caused by shortages was somewhat lessened by what one government official has called "legal thievery". By this he meant to illicit, but generally tolerated practice of trading in the so-called shadow economy, the prevalent underground system of private buying and selling of goods and services not otherwise available in the marketplace.

At a beach on the southern resort town of Sochi, swimmers and sunbathers enjoy themselves on a sunny Sunday afternoon. The facilities and amenities at Soviet resorts are rather poor by Western standards. The only meal I could find was a sausage served with crackers and a glob of mustard. The only drink available was some kind of orange soda served in plastic cups that looked they had just survived Stalingrad. Oddly, the concept of a picnic basket is unknown in the U.S.S.R. Most Crimean beaches are made of rocks and gravel but these children are enjoying the sand which was imported from Vietnam.
Photo by author

Yuri Andropov followed with a rigorous anti-corruption campaign aimed at stamping out black market profiteering. This policy has been adopted and strengthened under Gorbachev. It has not, however, affected the demand for passenger travel tickets. Summer vacation seems to be the bottom line under which Soviet citizens will not be dissuaded from wheeling and dealing.

Naturally, high placed employees in the travel industry are favorite friends to have. If one is not that fortunate, camping out in front of ticket offices or sneaking onto trains can also be resorted to. Driving is not usually a solution because the country is so large and doesn't have a developed highway system. The most popular resort areas in the Crimea are at least 1600 and 2050 kilometers away from Moscow and Leningrad respectively. Moreover, the small size of Soviet-made automobiles are simply not conducive to family travel.

Vladimir Shaposhnikov is an assistant director of an airline ticket office in central Smolensk. From morning to night his office is an endless stream of ticket seekers. "Some claim hardship and others claim emergency," he said in a rare moment of relative calm.

"Just yesterday I had three extra tickets to Odessa. There were nine people clamoring for them and no one had any more preference than anybody else. What would you do?" he asked. "I did what I had to. I told them to all go outside and settle it peacefully among themselves. I understand that they were seen arguing well past dark." After a brief pause he added, "I'm presuming that I haven't heard the last of it either."

No solutions have thus far placated an angry public. Despite the fact that the national railway operates 24 hours a day and the national airline, Aeroflot, is by far the world's largest, the demand for tickets is admittedly unmanageable. "Our problem is not supply, it's demand," said Shaposhnikov. "Everyone wants to travel from May through September. There simply aren't enough seats or beds to accommodate them all."

IT'S A DOG'S LIFE

Many Pets but No Pet Food in U.S.S.R.

Prior to the 1970's Soviet citizens living in major cities were discouraged from owning household pets, except tropical fish. The stated reason was the incompatibility of dogs and cats with the typical pint-sized apartment units in which 99 percent of all city-dwellers live.

As the acute housing shortage gradually decreased and communal bathrooms and kitchens became less common, the prohibition against house pets slowly atrophied. Today hundreds of thousands of Soviet households now include a dog or cat. Previously unavailable services such as veterinarian care and grooming parlors are now in business, although they have long waiting lists. Many cities now even have pet exhibitions, competitions and kennel clubs.

There's only one problem in the Soviet Union, there is no such thing as dog or cat food. In fact, with the exception of fish flakes and bird seed, the only feed available is for livestock. Soviet industry simply does not produce pet food and none has ever been imported. In a country that can't seem to provide enough food for its people, the absence of pet food has hardly become a compelling public issue. Its absence does, however, present a challenge to pet owners everywhere.

The manager of the Kiev Dog Market, Ludmilla Sirikova, explained that pet food is a luxury that they must do without. "When we have bread, meat and sugar shortages for workers, it is not possible to expect the production of pet food." The lack of food doesn't seem to bother her customers. According to Sirikova, quality dogs are in such great demand that her cages are always empty. "Pet food is no different than any other commodity," she said. "People just make do the best they can. We're used to it."

I'm guessing the country's pets don't know what they are missing. In the USA we can purchase all kinds of pet foods ranging from the humble can or slop to gourmet varieties that are quite pricey. Personally, I have never bonded with a dog or cat so I look at the large sum of dough required to feed pets as wasteful. In true Leninist fashion, I believe we'd all be better off devoting that money to feeding hungry people.

A BUYING NEW CAR TAKES PATIENCE OR LUCK

Couple Waits Six Years and a Long Day to Drive Away in Style

Smolensk: All of you who have pressed your noses against an auto showroom window lately or picked your way through the rebate offers in the Sunday newspaper, listen to the story of Gregory Ivanov and his new car.

Ivanov is one of the lucky ones, a war veteran, a recently retired pilot for the Soviet national airline Aeroflot, a man well placed for quick and privileged delivery. And it took only six years! That's six years from the date hi applied to purchase a new automobile and the morning when a little white postcard arrived at his apartment inviting him to pick up his new Zhiguli model 2014. And he ordered a number 2017. But he's satisfied, nevertheless.

Grigori and Natasha Ivanov photo
Photo by the author

Ivanov had to be at the dealer's showroom by 9 a.m. the next day with a certified check for 8,900 rubles. That's about $14,200. He had just three hours to get to his bank before it closed. He worried the bank clerks wouldn't honor his request for the money. In the U.S.S.R., any out of the ordinary activity at a bank is viewed with suspicion. A person can be interrogated for far less.

But Ivanov made it. And by 8:30 the next morning he and his wife Natasha took a taxi to the dealership and reported to window number 12, as directed in the card. He had been around long enough to know not to be late.

When he arrived, Ivanov was surprised to find that a long line of similarly-minded citizens waiting for their cars too. Once he got to the window, almost 90 minutes later, he was given a green form to complete. This entitled him to proceed to a door and another long line. Only a couple more hours and a few more bureaucrats stood between him and his shiny new Fiat-like automobile. By 11 a.m. he had filled out the last form and was ready to hand over his check in exchange for the keys and registration. When he heard his name called on a loudspeaker, he knew he was about to see what he had waited so long and impatiently for.

Well, not so fast. Six years before he ordered a blue model. Only green was available that day. Did he still want it?

That got me wondering, how does one purchase an automobile in the U.S.S.R.? So, I started my investigation by asking the man on the street. My first question: "Is there an automobile dealership around here?" It quickly became clear that the concept of an auto dealership is unknown here. Next, I asked the manager of the Novosti Press Agency auto fleet, a portly fellow who likes to nap in the backseat of his Volga sedan when not chauffeuring staff and guests around town. His name is Melor (which I learned stands for Mark, Engels, Lenin and October Revolution).

"You have to get lucky if you want to buy a new car for yourself," he said. "The most important thing is to get your name on a list with every factory you can identify. Then you have to enter the lotteries that they run in case you do get lucky and they pick your name. But everybody thinks the list and lotteries are rigged, so the best solution is to find a used car."

But then, where do you find a used car? "Everywhere, anywhere you can, he added. "You have to get the word out that you're looking and it'll come to you. Somebody will know somebody who knows somebody that can get you a car, even if it's a pile of crap."

How expensive are they? "Affordability is not really the problem. Most people have the cash (there is virtually no credit in the U.S.S.R.) because we don't have things to spend it on. But they are not cheap. A used car can cost the same or more than a new car due to their availability."

So, are used cars readily available? "No. They are hard to find, especially a good one. The best option is when your company or union is selling one. But then you have to be a on a list or win a lottery for those too."

Once you do purchase a car, how easy is it to get parts for it or to have it repaired? "That's tough too."

As I learned, city councils (called Soviets) operate repair facilities but they are always busy and it is difficult to schedule an appointment to get your care serviced. So, people do it themselves?

"Yes, everybody has a brother or a cousin who repairs cars for extra cash. But getting parts is very difficult. They are available on the black market or in flea markets. But like everything else, you have to get lucky."

It sounds like the best solution is to have a family member or a good friend who owns a car and knows how to get it serviced when needed. "Yes, that's the best. Unless you are like me and can use a car that belongs to your employer. That's the best solution."

STRANGE PROHIBITIONS AND GLASNOST SPUR NEW DEFIANCE

Will the Martial Arts Be Legalized?

A small group of like-minded men assembled recently in a Moscow gym. Their mission was simple: To formulate a concerted strategy to repeal a ban on the instruction, training or practice of karate in the Soviet Union.

The prohibition of karate and the other classical martial arts was ordered in 1982 because they were found to be, in the words of the national committee in charge of athletic competition, "murderous sports which are dangerous, abusive and anti-social." The banning of karate, as odd as it may seem in a nation as sports-minded as the U.S.S.R., is only one of a number of strange prohibitions which plague contemporary Soviet society.

For example:

- Men are prohibited from wearing shorts or cut-offs except on public beaches.
- The possession or transport of religious icons is a felony punishable by a fine, jail sentence or both.
- It is illegal to feed stray cats.
- It is against traffic rules for a driver to honk his horn unless it is an emergency situation.
- Citizens are prohibited from possessing foreign currency without a special permit.
- Until recently churches were prohibited from ringing their bells, despite of the fact that the Soviet Union has more historic cathedrals and bell towers than any other country in the world.

The purpose of these prohibitions, according to one Soviet journalist, is to seemingly further the public interest. He notes, for instance, that Soviet society has always maintained an unofficial dress code. "As for stray cats," he said, "there are so many in our city streets that feeding them only encourages their owners to let them run free."

In the past official prohibitions would have removed the matters from public discussion. However, in these days of liberalization more and more people are questioning what appear to be senseless rules and regulations. The karate enthusiasts are but one example of the emboldenment of Soviet citizens. Today thousands of newly organized groups are demanding changes in everything from menus in restaurants to official languages and flags. One group has even gone so far as to demand an end to the so-called special usage lanes on Soviet highways. Such lanes date back to Stalin's day and are restricted for use by Party and government vehicles only.

The Soviet journalist, who asked that his name not be disclosed, cautioned his remarks with the statement that many silly prohibitions are simply not enforced. "The suggestion that we live in a police state is a complete myth," he said. "Our police are simply too lazy to write-up citations for such things."

"That's misleading," interrupted his colleague. "Everyone knows that the uncertainty of our criminal system is enough to deter violations. The fact that a thing is silly or not doesn't enter into it," she said.

Irrespective of the nature of the prohibition, there seems to be no disagreement that the current mood of defiance is a result of President Mikhail Gorbachev's policy of openness, popularly known as Glasnost. Since it was first introduced three years ago, Glasnost has been singularly responsible for a plethora of changes in Soviet law and society. The contested elections held in the spring of 1989 and the convening of an ostensibly independent legislature during the summer are the two most significant.

But even the sudden openness cannot admit all truths, said the second journalist. "The fact that karate was banned is not due to danger. It's because the karate federation was so polluted with corruption that the authorities had no choice but to disband it entirely."

"Its Glasnost which will permit them to reintroduce it," she added.

PANDA-MONIUM

Animal Diplomacy Succeeds When Political Diplomacy Fails

Relations between the U.S.S.R. and the Peoples Republic of China have been at a standstill ever since Khrushchev was affronted by Mao over border disputes in the early 1960's. Mao was no doubt aching over the Russians' control over Communist Mongolia, China's unfriendly neighbor to the north. The Soviets were angry over Mao's constant "deviations" from Marxist-Leninist orthodoxy. Red Russia was not about to play second fiddle to Red China. The relationship deteriorated to such an extent under Brezhnev that the Soviet leader was reported to have contemplated launching a pre-emptive nuclear strike again in 1975 directed against China's hostility to an emergent Vietnam. The Soviets were no doubt prompted to act in response to Nixon's deft playing of the so-called "China Card" three years earlier. The thought of the USA and China establishing an Anti-Soviet alliance would presumably be enough to make the Kremlin consider anything.

Thankfully, cooler heads prevailed. Despite the Soviet Union's invasion and occupation of Afghanistan, acts the Chinese considered a gross violation of their tacit understanding about the balance of power in northern Asia, the relationship gradually warmed - most probably because China's weapons in the hands of the Muhjahadeen guerrillas helped to kick Russian butt. To assuage the Kremlin's upset China did

Pandas Ping-Ping and Tsing-Tsing frolic at the Moscow Zoo. Photo courtesy of Pravda.

what it always does when it wants to cozy up to an enemy - it sent a pair of panda bears.

Just as Ling-Ling and Hsing-Hsing warmed the hearts of Americans when they first arrived in at the National Zoo in Washington, D.C. in 1972, Ping-Ping and Tsing-Tsing have similarly melted decades of wrangling between the two Communist giants. Ensconced in a newly constructed exhibit at the Moscow Zoo, the panda pair are now its biggest draw. One cannot help but notice that a short time later a deputy Soviet foreign minister flew to Beijing for the first high-level talks between them in eighteen years.

What is it about these amazing animals that possesses them of such diplomatic power? Is this a secret ancient Chinese pacification tactic?

Pandas are very unique, and very cute creatures its true. They live in the bamboo trees of China's Yunnan and Szechwan provinces and possess an unusual sixth finger, more a second-thumb which has evolved from their wrist bone. It is a perfect example of nature's power of adapting animals to their environments. Pandas are vegetarians and can grow to weigh over 1200 pounds. They are passive and playful. They are ideal zoo fare. Yet they remain an endangered species. The World Wildlife Fund has adopted the panda as its emblem.

As I strolled through the old Moscow Zoo, waiting in yet another line to glimpse Ping and Tsing in action, I couldn't help but wonder what a silly race we are too. Millions of Americans, Japanese and Europeans have waited with expectation as expert zoologists have attempted to assist captive pandas to reproduce. Extraordinary measures costing millions of dollars have been employed to assure the survival of the species. Pandas have symbolized something that universally touches man's heart. It's an effort a whole lot more sensible than building bombs.

I think the Chinese are on to something.

ADVENTURES AT THE NEW AGE SUMMIT

A Fantasy in One Act

At the Moscow Summit between President Ronald Regan and President Mikhail Gorbachev (May 1988), nobody knew where the karma would bounce. Hard-nosed bargaining was inevitable; each leader came armed with precise, secret knowledge. The fate of the world might depend on this summit, so each man was determined to press his advantage. The questions were fierce; the answers deep and technical.

"Say," said Reagan, "aren't you a Pisces?"

Gorbachev chuckled. "Aren't you being an ignoramus?"

"No, I'm Aquarius," said Ron. "And I'm serious: the stars rule our lives. Believe me, I should know...I worked in Hollywood!

Gorby looked intently at Ron, unable to decide if he was joking or not. Regan gestured toward the heavens.

"There are cosmic forces all around us, and... well, tell me, Mikhail... haven't you ever felt you were being guided by some all-powerful force?"

"Yes, the Central Committee," Gorbachev smiled broadly, but Reagan's face remained serious. Gorbachev composed himself. "Of what advantage is it, knowing these things?"

"Well, Mikhail, astrology can show you your destiny. It tells you when to do important things—like withdrawing from Afghanistan. When I bombed Libya, Khadafy's karma sure got worse!" Reagan chuckled. "You see, it's all in the timing. Heck, I divorced my first wife by using astrology!"

Reagan's face again got serious. "Maybe I should try it on Ed Meese."

Gorbachev changed the subject. "Mr. President, about our treaty..."

"Oh yes, the INF treaty ... that's the one we're destined to sign. I know because Nancy's personal psychic reader saw it happening. She said we should cut our missiles 50% because otherwise the space people from Alpha Centauri would be very angry, and I don't want to rile the six-armed, three-headed beings on Alpha Centauri—do you, Mikhail?"

Gorbachev rolled his eyes. "Oh, certainly not, Mr. President, certainly not."

"Well," said Ronnie, "here's what I think. We'll make our reductions into a nice round number so Nancy's numerologist will be happy. We'll figure out the number after Nancy talks long-distance to him."

Gorbachev was squirming. "Mr. President, may I make a frank comment?"

"Well, of course, Mikhail, but after that, can I read your palm?"

"Fine." Gorbachev got up from his upholstered chair and strode toward the window. Despite his polished manner, Gorby was highly agitated. He had problems of his own, both foreign and domestic. Did Reagan realize how much money it was taking to keep Raisa in furs?

He whirled sharply around. "Mr. President, about your support for the Nicaraguan Contras..." Gorbachev's voice trailed off. Reagan was sitting in full lotus pose on the chair, and was now wearing an amethyst crystal on his neck. Cosmic Ron opened his eyes and smiled.

"Mikhail, I've just had a vision of our past lives. We were two leaders in 10,000 B.C. who got mad at each other and blew up the lost continent of Atlantis. I think we came back this time to rectify things. So, I'm going to drop my Star Wars research and become a vegetarian. What about you? You could get rid of that birthmark if you ate macrobiotic."

Gorbachev gave in. "All right! All right! I'll do anything! I'll let the Jews emigrate! I'll let go of Eastern Europe! I'll tear down the Berlin

Wall with my own hands! Just stop torturing me!" He collapsed in his chair, holding his head with his shaking hands.

Reagan just smiled his right-brained, beatific smile. "Don't worry, Mikhail, it's all the Divine Plan. (Though I'll probably catch hell from Pat Robertson!) Say, would you like to meet one of Nancy's friends? She channels Jesus, Buddha, Saint Germain, and a 2000-year old Jewish garment salesman."

Gorbachev raised his head. A slight smile hovered about his lips. "You know, Ron, I think I would. May I invite Raisa?"

"Of course. What spirit would she like to meet?"

Robert Cost, founder and president of the Wisconsin Military History Museum, with a Soviet Army T-34 tank donated by the Soviet Ministry of Defense. Photo by Jim Brozek courtesy of Soviet Life.

TANKS A MILLION

Old Soviet Tanks Deployed Far Afield

Now that the Warsaw Pact has ceased to exist; now that the U.S. and the U.S.S.R. have agreed to sweeping reductions in conventional forces in Europe; now that the Red Army has come undone, the question arises: What's to be done with all those Soviet tanks?

While many are being destroyed outright, in accordance with treaty obligations, a hundred thousand other T-21's, T-34's and T-38 Soviet tanks are being used for a myriad of tasks in many places throughout the world. The non-communist government of Czechoslovakia is converting its arsenal of Soviet-made tanks into an arsenal of fire engines. Poland is deploying them as snow plows and road graders. Romania sold 25 to Brazil to be used as bulldozers. In the Soviet Union itself many tanks have been transferred to construction and river dredging crews due to a shortage of more appropriate vehicles.

As Soviet Military Attaché, Major General Nikolai Zlenko reluctantly pointed out, comparatively few are deployed for military purposes outside the Soviet Union. This is due to the Soviet's inability to furnish spare parts to maintain them. The nation's military-industrial capability has been sucked down the same drain as the entire national economy. Operational tank production facilities are now about as rare as functioning toothpaste factories. But then again, in a nation where the number of tanks exceeded the number of public toilets, finding non-threatening uses for a T-34 is no easy matter.

Germany, ever-anxious to remove any further traces of the Red Army from its soil, has agreed to purchase four thousand Soviet tanks. It's expected they'll be recycled, though several are known to have been shipped to Israel where they'll undoubtedly be put to some ghastly use. This is somewhat understandable for a country that just finished melting down seventy tons of useless East German coinage. Several African countries, former clients of the Soviets, have abandoned their old tanks altogether not having parts or fuel to keep them operable. It is said that from the air one can spot old T-18's and armored personnel carriers littered in the wilderness. Doubtless others have been deployed as barricades around besieged presidential palaces and police headquarters. In Egypt, vendors are selling bits of Soviet tank metal as souvenirs of the Cold War.

Being endlessly in need of foreign currency, the floundering Soviet government has resorted to auctioning off old tanks to the highest bidder. The U.S. cautioned the Soviets to be sure none would be sold or trans-shipped to Iraq, which has an abundance of spare parts thanks to the U.S. Air Force during the Gulf War. Feeling isolated, no doubt, North Korea has reportedly recently purchased a couple of hundred tanks at deep discounts. A couple of dozen have been bartered to Vietnam and Laos in exchange for rice and tea. Still others have been sold as scrap iron to South Korea and Japan.

One of the most creative uses the Soviets have found for their old tanks is donating them to military museums. Thus far complete tanks have been donated to museums in the U.S., Norway, Finland and Australia. It's no surprise the Soviets insist on delivering the gifts themselves, for currency of course.

Part VI
THE HUNT FOR GORBACHEV'S HOUSE

The new presidential residence on Kosygin Highway high above Moscow in a district called Lennin Hills. A Zil limousine with all four doors open was parked behind the gates, as if ready to receive Gorby himself. Two other unmarked vehicles occupied by presidential security officers were on guard at the foot of the driveway. They would not permit their photograph to be taken.
Photo by the author

THE HUNT FOR GORBACHEV'S HOUSE

How I Confirmed the Location of the New Executive Residence

Anyone who has had the opportunity to take a leisurely drive around Moscow knows that apart from the central district bounded between Red Square, Kalinin Avenue, Dzerzhinsky Square and the Marx Avenue, the balance of the city is a faceless urban sprawl. Popular attractions such as Gorky Park, Arbat Street, the Exhibition of Economic Achievements and the city's historic architectural jewels are lost in a web of thoroughfares and concentric circles around which the city grew.

For this reason, an offer to view the city from the heights of the Lenin Hills is a particular treat. Located in the southeastern sector of the city, the Lenin Hills are the seat of Moscow State University and the central research laboratory for the U.S.S.R. Academy of Sciences. It's clear air and tree lined streets contrast markedly with the potpourri of squares, prospekts and parks which flare out in all directions below. In the foregoing stands Luzhniki Stadium, the site of the 1980 Summer Olympics, and more recently of rallies and political discussion conclaves marking the opening session of the newly elected Congress of Peoples' Deputies. Beyond this, along the course of the winding river which gave the Soviet capital its name, are the shining golden domes of the Kremlin.

"While we're here," asked my guide Alexi, "do you want to see Gorbachev's new house?" One can imagine my response. "You mean Gorbachev lives up here?" I asked.

"Yes, they've only recently opened a new presidential residence, but nobody is supposed to know about it. They don't advertise such things here," Alexi said.

"Let's go!"

We drove slowly along the former Rosimovsky Highway, a clean, quiet boulevard just beyond the university campus gates. On the right-hand side, behind high walls and thick trees stand a series of old and new buildings which were all unknown to our driver. It was at that point that we noticed a squatty white Lada automobile not far behind us, likewise hugging the right-hand side of the road and moving slowly.
We continued forward until we stopped in front of a dark, modern looking five-story building with a gate and guardhouse at the front of the driveway.

Alexi whispered a few words in Russian to the driver and we exited. Our car sped ahead about two hundred yards and came to rest all alone at what appeared to be the end of the block. Alexi and I, with my camera, approached the guardhouse. We were surprised to find it empty.

"This is the apartment house of the Politburo," Alexi said. I looked up and noticed what appeared to be eight apartment units, two per floor, each with a long balcony surrounding it. The ground floor is presumably a reception area, undoubtedly equipped with a special canteen stocked with goods which are unavailable elsewhere. There were no television cameras or security devices in sight. Then Alexi said, "Kosygin (the former Soviet premier) and Suslov (the former chief party ideologist) used to live here. That's why they've renamed this street Kosygin Highway."

Just then a middle-aged man approached us. He identified himself as the doorman, although his grimy black hands and mechanic's coat clearly showed he was working on an automobile engine. We had obviously disturbed him. He entered the guardhouse and locked the door behind him. In a moment he reappeared, but now he donned a fancy looking military-style hat.

"What do you need?" he said. Alexi identified himself as a Novosti Press Agency journalist and displayed his pocket-sized credentials.

"We're taking a tour of the area," he said. "This gentleman (referring to me) is an American writer researching Moscow's architecture. What is this house?"

"If you are looking for the Institute of Chemical Engineering, it's over there," and the man pointed in the direction from which we came. I could see the white Lada sitting on the side of the road, it's three occupants remaining still.

He continued, "This is just a support building housing offices for the institute."

I looked at Alexi and in English asked if the guard was telling the truth. Alexi shook his head prudently.

"Why do you have a gate and guardhouse here then?" I asked.

The man ignored my question and glanced at Alexi. "Do you mind if I take a photograph of the building?" I asked.

"Do as you like, but I can't let you onto the grounds," he answered.

I carefully took two shots. Alexi and I then continued up the sidewalk. The man entered the guardhouse and watched us as we cleared the estate grounds. He wasn't the only one keeping an eye on us. The little white Lada crept along 20 yards behind us. "He is probably right," said Alexi. "That house probably is in the name of the Institute of Chemical Engineering, but that is exactly how they mask things like this, so nobody knows."

It was warm and a clear afternoon and the mild breeze at our backs pointed us forward; anxiety dissuaded us from looking back.

The next building we came to was obviously brand new. It was a four-story structure of crème colored block with thick brown window casements. Unlike the others we had passed, it was plainly visible from the street and was separated from it by a short stretch of lawn and a six-foot high black iron fence. It was much less forbidding than the fence which surrounds the White House.

"This is it," said Alexi. "Gorbachev's new home." I looked up and wondered if it was possible. Somehow it didn't fit my expectations. Perhaps it was because, although it is large, it's really rather ordinary. There were no guards or dogs, or anything even remotely menacing to protect it. In an instant, my doubts subsided. There in the distance of the long driveway, behind the gates was an unmistakable symbol of Kremlinogical privilege; a Zil limousine, standing with all four doors open as if ready to receive its owner.

Suddenly behind us, a shiny black Volga sedan pulled up in front of the driveway. It had a high antenna protruding from the trunk and four male occupants. The two near side doors sprang open. Alexi froze. I could see the fright in his face. The man in the rear seat wore a shoulder holster that was clearly visible, but he remained seated, only extending his right foot to the ground. He was obviously the one in charge.

I looked at him and suddenly realized we were all alone. Apart from our waiting car ahead, the Volga and the Lada still behind us, the street barren of automobile or pedestrian traffic.

Not knowing what to do, I showed my camera to the man, as if to say, "I'm only here to take a picture." He did not acknowledge my gesture. He and his colleagues sat motionless and staring. Alexi then looked at me. Undaunted. I raised the camera to my eye, focused and snapped a single photograph. I turned around again. Not a stir from the Volga. In the Lada, the three pairs of eyes remained still too.

"Come on," said Alexi, "let's go." We walked warily past the front of the house. Its design consists of two side facades each with twelve covered windows, and a central curved semi-portico entrance with a simple flat canopy over the front door.

I looked back at the Volga. Nothing had changed. The car and its occupants were as motionless as the curtains covering the windows in the house.

When we got to the end of the building, I could see the fence extend far into the rear, only now it was higher. I quickly snapped two more photographs.

"Let's go, now!" he said. We caught up to our car, buckled our seat belts and proceeded down the street. I could see our driver looking in his rear-view mirror. Sure enough, the white Lada began following us. Alexi looked back in horror.

He said the Russian equivalent to "Uh, oh!"

Being in the back seat, I refused to turn around for fear of giving ourselves away. Journalist Nick Daniloff's account of his captivity by the K.G.B. in 1986, a book which I had read immediately preceding my journey, popped into my head. It was not a comforting thought.

Then Alexi said to the driver, "Turn around and go the other way." At a U-turn in the boulevard, he did so. The Lada followed us, but remained comfortably behind. We knew we were being followed and they knew we knew it. As we repassed Gorbachev's house, the six eyes from the

Volga followed us too. "Turn right up here," said Alexi. Our driver flicked on his blinkers and the Lada sped up behind us. I finally turned around and saw it had its blinkers on too.

Now I began to worry. I knew that anything could happen now.

We made our turn, slowly. Victor, our driver, heaved a sigh of relief when the Lada continued onward. I quickly turned to see it pass. My eyes hit the eyes of the front seat passenger for an instant, then he was gone.

Alexi looked at me. I could see that he was more relieved than Victor or I. Of course, we both knew that if we had been stopped, or worse, arrested, he would be in far more trouble than me.

Then, in an instance, the black Volga pulled up directly behind us. We turned right at the next corner. It did too. Alexi nonchalantly turned his head and looked behind us.

"It's them," he said. He paused for a moment. "If they wanted to stop us, they would have done it by now."

"Turn left up here," he told the driver. Victor swerved over to the left-hand lane and made a sharp turn directly in front of an oncoming truck; an oncoming truck that would have struck me first! But the risk was worth it. The black Volga immediately became locked out and had no choice but to continue forward.

A feeling of exaltation filled our car. Victor started to laugh. We had ducked the K.G.B. We all laughed, perhaps more out of relief than joy.

After a moment I said, "Okay, Alexi, how do I get confirmation that that was really Mikhail and Raisa Gorbachev's new house." He turned around and looked squarely at me in disbelief.

Since the days of Stalin, the Soviet party and governmental leadership are widely known to have state-owned dachas at their disposal. But even former President Leonid Brezhnev never had a house within the city. It was widely known that he maintained an apartment off of Kutuzov Prospekt, near the Triumphal Arch on the historic battlefield of Poklonnya Hill. The daily race of Zils to and from the Kremlin and the building where he and his successor Yuri Andropov was also said to reside, proved irrefutable evidence of the fact.

"Gorbachev wanted an official presidential mansion," Alexi said. "Though it's not publicized, we know that's where it is. Novosti knows these things for certain. You can take my word."

Then, it hit me. I remembered reading in Hendrick Smith's book *The Russians*, that some western analysts believed Novosti Press Agency is really just a public arm of the Ministry of Internal Affairs. Could it be true? Had I just been set up to scare me out of my boots? It was, after all, at Alexi's suggestion that we visit the house.

I thought about it for a while. This was my third day of a trip around the Soviet Union which was to last almost two months. Did they want this incident to serve as a warning to me to be on my best (and least inquisitive) behavior? I knew that at least, in the past, stranger things had happened.

In any event, I was glad to obtain what I thought was a genuine scoop. Information as seemingly innocuous as this is of great interest to American Sovietologists. It brought to mind a story I had heard of how the Central Intelligence Agency had tried in vain to obtain a sample of Gorbachev's feces for medical analysis while he was visiting the U.S. last December. Whether it's true or not, I can't say. Based on the joke that is currently circling the country, the Soviets seem to believe it.

Over the period of the following six weeks, I feverishly attempted to get verification that the house I had photographed on Kosygin Highway was indeed Gorbachev's new residence.

Several cab drivers I asked confirmed that they frequently see lines of speeding Zils enter the gates. Others I asked denied any knowledge of the subject. A seasonal tourist guide named Irina disagreed. "I've heard people talking about it, but I doubt it," she said. "If *Time* magazine can't find the house, what makes you think you did."

In a published interview in the May issue of the *Journal News of the Soviet Communist Party Central Committee*, Gorbachev said he had an apartment in the city and a state-owned dacha "equipped with the appropriate features". Then he added, "The Central Committee and the government also have at their disposal special buildings in which distinguished guests from abroad are received or which are used for other official purposes."

I decided to contact every Soviet who I could fairly describe as being "in the know." I visited the Facilities Administration building of Moscow State University, but it was closed due to summer vacation. I then managed to find the building services department attached to the local District Soviet (council). I requested an appointment with the director general to ask a few questions about the area's newer construction projects.

After a short wait in a crowded reception area, I was invited into his office. He was a tall, good looking man dressed informally. He greeted me warmly and got back down at his traditional T-shaped desk, standard issue to upper-echelon bureaucrats. There were chairs lining the sides of his spacious office. I was later informed that these were for citizens who wished to lodge complaints to the director in person. Apparently, he makes each complainant sit through the litany of grievances that people bring to him in the hope of impressing each subsequent complainant with a degree of understanding of the multitude of problems that he is asked to solve.

"What can I do for you today?" asked the director general. "As you can see I am very busy and don't have too much time to spend with you."

I began, "Can you tell me whether the large new house on Kosygin Highway (apparently it does not have an address) belongs to President Gorbachev?"

"Which new house?"

"The one directly next to the offices of the Institute of Chemical Engineering," I said. A sly smile crossed his face. "No."

"Pardon me sir, I don't understand. No, what?" I asked. "No. I cannot tell you," he said. Then he smiled again. "Is that all you wanted to know?"

"Yes, that's all. I think it is," I said. "I saw a limousine in the driveway and there were guards out in front."

"When did you go there?"

"I was there just an hour ago, and two times before that." I replied.

The Director's eyes opened wide. He pushed a button on the speaker box on his desk. The voice of one of his secretaries answered.

He then said something in Russian too fast for me to understand, but the tone of astonishment in his voice was unmistakable. He looked at the business card I handed him when I first entered his office.

"If that's all Mr.—" he said as he garbled my name. Seeing that this was my last chance, I quickly blurted out.

"Are you saying you do not know if that's Gorbachev's house or you're not sure - or it is, but you can't confirm it?"

He looked at me with a stillness in his manner. I was afraid he didn't understand my Russian phrasing of the question.

"I didn't understand what you said," he said. "There's nothing I can do for you. You have to go to the Central Committee to get any information."

With that he politely escorted me out of his office and wished me good luck. He closed the door behind me, obviously not wishing to see any of the throng who were still waiting to see him. I've been to the Soviet Union enough times to know that getting any information from the Central Committee headquarters in the Kremlin is impossible. If I were lucky enough to get through the gates, I would certainly be referred to the press office of the Foreign Ministry. Having been there only two days before, I knew enough to decline the advice.

Moscow in August is no different from Washington DC. Things grind to a halt while the government takes a holiday. Feeling frustrated at not having obtained ironclad journalistic confirmation, I decided to drop the matter. Maybe I can sell the photos to the National Enquirer, I thought.

On the eve of my departure, two days later the unlikely happened. I was having dinner with my Novosti Press Agency colleagues and several of their guests. Having spent a month and a half touring their country, they were curious to hear my overall impression. As hour

Tatiana Vysotskaya's model-like good looks hide a mind that is first-rate. Meeting her unexpectedly both solved a mystery and capped my fellowship on a high note. The last I heard she was finishing her graduate degree in advanced policy studies and was hoping to find a job within Russia's Ministry of Environmental Affairs.
Photo by the author

after hour and toast after toast proceeded, I came back to the matter of Gorbachev's house. Then the woman sitting at my left, Tatiana, a delightfully friendly woman who happens to be a clerk of the Presidium of the Academy of Sciences, said she was certain that the building in question was really Gorbachev's new home.

Realizing this was the information I was after, I quickly asked her to dance. Having earlier told Tatiana that she had a "smile worth a million bucks" she readily accepted my offer. The restaurant band played another non-descript pop song. I said I was tired and wanted to slow dance.

"How do you know for certain?" I asked.

"Because my boss met him there last month. He told me all about it."

"Who is your boss?"

She provided the name but I was in no position to write it down. What I do remember her saying is that he is one of the five permanent secretaries of the Presidium, which is the executive body of the academy. She told me that the leadership of the Presidium was invited to lunch with Gorbachev for a meeting on environmental policy. She said her boss described the furnishings and food as being first rate.

"Meeting Gorbachev is a big thing, even to him," she said. "I was even in his office when he talked to his wife about it on the telephone."

Feeling triumphant, I asked her to dance to another song. Tatiana readily agreed. She said she relished the opportunity to practice speaking English. I relished listening to her.

She added details as they occurred to her. I wished I had had my mini-cassette recorder in my pocket.

About the Author

Author of *Who Said That?* and more than a dozen books and plays, J. Ajlouny holds a B.A. in Journalism from Wayne State University and a J.D. from Michigan State University. He founded the Federal Bureau of Entertainment (FBE) to develop and produce one-person stage shows featuring prominent British actors. Now focusing on touring theatre projects and Great Lakes history research, he is a writer and editor of humor, pop-reference, essays, and assorted arcania. He lives in Detroit.

Fresh Ink Group

Publishing
Free Memberships
Share & Read Free Stories, Essays, Articles
Free-Story Newsletter
Writing Contests

❧

Books
E-books
Amazon Bookstore

❧

Authors
Editors
Artists
Professionals
Publishing Services
Publisher Resources

❧

Members' Websites
Members' Blogs
Social Media

Email: info@FreshInkGroup.com
Twitter: @FreshInkGroup
Google+: Fresh Ink Group
Facebook.com/FreshInkGroup
LinkedIn: Fresh Ink Group
About.me/FreshInkGroup

FreshInkGroup.com

Who Said That? provides an entertaining and authoritative reference for the origins and meanings of our common figures of speech.

- Who said 100+ famous expressions?
- Who *really* said them?
- What did they actually say?
- What did they actually mean?
- Why did they say them that way?
- Who repeated what was said?

Surprisingly true, sometimes strange, always fascinating, the stories about whence came these expressions will entertain, educate, and even amaze you.

Fresh Ink Group

A "Figure of speech" is an expression that creates a more forceful or dramatic meaning, such as "stretch the truth" or "baptism by fire." We finally have a thesaurus to discover their origins and the sources of their meanings. Whether reading it for fun, researching phrases you use, or studying the symbolic foundations of our language, Figuratively Speaking is the resource you'll reach for time and again.

Fresh Ink Group

In this boisterous but sensitive drama, playwright J. Ajlouny looks beyond public image to find the heart of this young woman thrust wildly into fame as a sex symbol. *Marilyn, Norma Jean and Me* weaves biography with humor to explore the movie star's widely speculated plan to leave Hollywood for Broadway. The author imagines her innocence and vulnerability, her friendliness and loyalty, even as the public image threatens to steal her humanity. This play is a must-see or -read for its powerful way of finding the real Norma Jean in the legend known as Marilyn Monroe.

Push Pull Press/Fresh Ink Group

Much has been explored about Shakespeare and his life, but little is known about how this small-town boy with a grammar-school education came to pen masterworks like *Hamlet* and *King Lear*. In *Meet William Shakespeare*, playwright J. Ajlouny creates authentic and plausible explanations that answer centuries-old questions about the man and his work. The result is an educational and fun portrait of Shakespeare, as told by The Bard himself.

Push Pull Press/Fresh Ink Group

Few men have endured the indignity of having their very existence challenged as thoroughly as William Shakespeare, late of Stratford-upon-Avon. From scholars to amateur enthusiasts, many cannot bring themselves to believe he wrote his own body of work. Playwright J. Ajlouny presents the arguments for and against, all statements and proofs drawn from the historical record. Everybody must decide for himself, but *The Trial of William Shakespeare* makes the controversy both intriguing and fun.

Push Pull Press/Fresh Ink Group

www.ingramcontent.com/pod-product-compliance
Lightning Source LLC
Chambersburg PA
CBHW061642040426
42446CB00010B/1535